THE REMINISCENCES OF
Admiral Harold Page Smith
U.S. Navy (Retired)

INTERVIEWED BY
Paul Stillwell

U.S. Naval Institute • Annapolis, Maryland

Copyright © 2014

Preface

Admiral Smith had a long and distinguished naval career. It spanned nearly 45 years in uniform from his induction at the Naval Academy in 1920 until President Lyndon Johnson presented him with the Distinguished Service Medal upon the admiral's retirement in 1965. He witnessed vast change in the naval service over those years and rose to its highest rank. During his final tour of service, he was one of only six four-star admirals on the active roster.

Despite urging that he do an oral history on his entire career, Admiral Smith declined. As he explained in a letter of 5 August 1991, "Almost all the events of my life that I regard as important are highlighted by my view of the incompetence of others. I couldn't tell my story with any honesty if I failed to state fully my memory of such failures. So, with regret, I shall not agree to an interview." The good news was that he had by that point done oral history interviews on two of his tours of duty—service as a junior officer in the battleship *Arizona* (BB-39) in 1928-29 and command of the battleship *Missouri* (BB-63) in 1949-50. Some of the contents of those interviews appeared in my books on those two ships, and a portion of the *Missouri* interview was excerpted as an article, "The Value of Confidence," *Naval History*, Fall 1991, page 36.

Further good news is that fact that the admiral frequently went off on tangents from the battleship-specific interviews and discussed other tours of duty as well. He strayed to discuss his service in the fleet auxiliary ship *Procyon* (AG-11), destroyer duty in the brand-new *Farragut* (DD-348), command of the four-piper *Stewart* (DD-224) in action against the Japanese early in World War II, and command of Destroyer Squadron Four near the end of the war. In duty following the war, he talked about service as chief of staff to Commander Destroyer Force Atlantic Fleet and various Pentagon billets. He recalled being Chief of Naval Personnel when Fleet Admiral Chester Nimitz made a touching visit to Smith's office following the funeral of Fleet Admiral William Halsey.

Much of the content of the two interviews has remained unpublished until now and should be of interest to scholars and other readers. In preparing the material for publication, I have done some light editing for the sake of accuracy, clarity, and smoothness, and I have added footnotes to provide additional information for the benefit of readers. Finally, I have indexed the contents to facilitate retrieval. Ms. Janis Jorgensen of the Naval Institute staff has coordinated the printing and binding of the finished product.

In completing this volume, the Naval Institute expresses its gratitude to the Tawani Foundation and the Pritzker Military Library of Chicago for their generous financial support of the oral history program that produced this memoir.

Paul Stillwell
U.S. Naval Institute
March 2013

ADMIRAL HAROLD PAGE SMITH
UNITED STATES NAVY (RETIRED)

A native of Mobile, Alabama, Admiral Smith graduated from the Naval Academy with the class of 1924. His early service included sea duty on board the battleships *Idaho* (BB-42), *Arizona* (BB-39), *Nevada* (BB-36), and the cargo ship *Procyon* (AG-11); three years as gunnery officer of the destroyer *Farragut* (DD-348); and two tours of shore duty, first as Spanish instructor at the Naval Academy, and later as progress officer at the Naval Gun Factory, Washington, D.C.

Ordered to the Asiatic Station in June 1939, he served for nine months as engineer officer of the cruiser *Marblehead* (CL-12), and at the outbreak of World War II was commanding officer of the *Stewart* (DD-224), a destroyer operating off Borneo. Under his command the *Stewart* participated in the Java Sea campaign, escorted the stricken *Marblehead* to safety, and took part in sweeps into Makassar Strait and troop convoy duty before her damage by Japanese cruiser gunfire during the assault on Bali Island. He was awarded the Navy Cross for "exceptionally meritorious conduct . . . during a night engagement on February 19-20, 1942 . . . " and received the Bronze Lion from Queen Wilhelmina of the Netherlands in recognition of his skillful and gallant action in combat.

After the loss of the *Stewart*, he served on the staff of the Commander in Chief U.S. Fleet (War Plans Section), attending the Combined Staff conferences in Washington and Quebec, Canada, and for a month was a member of General Dwight Eisenhower's plans staff in North Africa. In 1943-44 he commanded Destroyer Division Seven and later Destroyer Squadron Four, which was assigned variously to the Third and Fifth fleets, the British Eastern Fleet, and the Marianas Command. He was twice awarded the Legion of Merit, with Combat V, for outstanding services in recognition of his skillful and gallant action in combat.

Following the war, he served successively as Navy member of the Joint War Plans Committee, Joint Chiefs of Staff, and as assistant for United Nations affairs in the office of the Assistant Chief of Naval Operations (International Affairs). In February 1949 he assumed command of the battleship *Missouri* (BB-63), and from December of that year to August 1950 served on the staff of Commander Destroyer Force Atlantic Fleet, with brief additional duty in command of that force, and from February to April 1950 in command of the *Missouri*. He next served as Deputy Chief of Information, Navy Department, and in December 1951 became Director, Office of Foreign Military Affairs, Office of the Secretary of Defense.

Sea duty as Commander Amphibious Group Two preceded his consecutive assignments as Assistant Comptroller, Director of Budget and Reports, Navy Department, and Deputy Comptroller of the Navy. He was chief of staff and aide to the Supreme Allied Commander Atlantic from 23 October 1956 until January 1958, when he assumed duty as Chief of Naval Personnel, Chief of the Bureau of Naval Personnel, and Deputy Chief of Naval Operations (Personnel and Naval Reserve), Navy Department.

Admiral Smith was relieved as Chief of Naval Personnel in February 1960 and became Commander in Chief U.S. Naval Forces Eastern Atlantic and Mediterranean on 18 February 1960, with the rank of admiral. On 1 March 1960, with the reorganization of all U.S. forces in Europe, Admiral Smith became Commander in Chief U.S. Naval Forces Europe, retaining as additional duty his assignment as CinCNELM, with further additional duty as naval component commander of the U.S. European Command, and (designated by the Joint Chiefs of Staff) as Specified Commander for all U.S. Naval Forces in the Middle East. In March 1963 he was ordered to duty as Commander in Chief Atlantic and U.S. Atlantic Fleet and Supreme Allied Commander Atlantic, the latter a NATO post. He was relieved of the three simultaneous billets on 30 April 1965 and retired from active duty on 1 May 1965.

Family and Personal Data:

Born:	Mobile, Alabama, 17 February 1904
Parents:	Harvey Samuel and Elizabeth Warren Smith
Wife:	Former Helen Dee Rogers of Oklahoma City, Oklahoma
Children:	None
Education;	University Military School, Mobile; U.S. Naval Academy, class of 1924
Died:	Virginia Beach, Virginia, 4 January 1993

Dates of Rank:

5 June 1924	Ensign
5 June 1927	Lieutenant (Junior Grade)
30 June 1933	Lieutenant
1 April 1939	Lieutenant Commander
20 August 1942	Commander (Temporary)
1 August 1980	Captain (Temporary), 6 November 1943
7 August 1947	Captain, to rank from 1 June 1943
1 January 1952	Rear Admiral (Temporary)
1 July 1954	Rear Admiral, to rank from 1 January 1952
24 October 1956	Vice Admiral
18 February 1960	Admiral

Decorations and Medals:
Distinguished Service Medal
Navy Cross
Legion of Merit with combat V
Gold star in lieu of second Legion of Merit with Combat V
American Defense Service Medal
American Campaign Medal
European-African-Middle Eastern Campaign Medal

Asiatic-Pacific Campaign Medal
World War II Victory Medal
Navy Occupation Service Medal, Asia clasp
China Service Medal
National Defense Service Medal
Philippine Defense Ribbon
Expert Rifleman Medal
Expert Pistol Shot Medal
Netherlands Order of the Bronze Lion

Chronological Record of Service:

Jul 1924-Jun 1925	USS *Idaho* (BB-42)
Jun 1925-Apr 1928	USS *Procyon* (AG-11)
Apr 1928-Jul 1929	USS *Arizona* (BB-39)
Jul 1929-Jun 1931	USS *Nevada* (BB-36)
Jun 1931-May 1934	U.S. Naval Academy, Annapolis, Maryland, Spanish instructor
May 1934-Jun 1937	USS *Farragut* (DD-348)
Jun 1937-Jun 1939	Naval Gun Factory, Washington, D.C., progress officer
Jun 1939-May 1940	USS *Marblehead* (CL-12), engineer officer
May 1940-Feb 1942	USS *Stewart* (DD-224), commanding officer
Feb 1942-Mar 1942	U.S. Naval Forces, Southwest Pacific
Mar 1942-Sep 1943	Staff, Commander in Chief U.S. Fleet, Washington, D.C., War Plans Section
Sep 1943-Apr 1944	Commander Destroyer Division Seven
Apr 1944-Sep 1945	Commander Destroyer Squadron Four
Sep 1945-Jan 1949	Office of the Chief of Naval Operations (Navy Member, Joint War Plans Committee, Joint Chiefs of Staff)
Feb 1949-Dec 1949	USS *Missouri* (BB-63), commanding officer
Dec 1949-Oct 1950	Destroyer Force Atlantic Fleet, chief of staff and aide

Feb 1950-Apr 1950	USS *Missouri* (BB-63), temporary additional duty as commanding officer
Oct 1950-Dec 1951	Office of the Secretary of the Navy, Deputy Chief of Information
Dec 1951-Nov 1953	Office of the Secretary of Defense, Director, Office of Foreign Military Affairs
Nov 1953-Feb 1955	Commander Amphibious Group Two
Feb 1955-Jan 1956	Office of the Comptroller of the Navy, Assistant Comptroller, Director of Budget and Reports
Jan 1956-Oct 1956	Deputy Comptroller of the Navy
Oct 1956-Dec 1957	Staff, Supreme Allied Commander Atlantic, chief of staff and aide
Jan 1958-Feb 1960	Chief of Naval Personnel, Chief of the Bureau of Naval Personnel, and Deputy Chief of Naval Operations (Personnel and Reserve)
Feb 1960-Apr 1963	Commander in Chief U.S. Naval Forces Eastern Atlantic and Mediterranean; title changed on 1 March 1960 to Commander in Chief U.S. Naval Forces Europe with additional duty as Commander in Chief U.S. Naval Forces Eastern Atlantic and Mediterranean
Apr 1963-Apr 1965	Commander in Chief U.S. Atlantic Command and U.S. Atlantic Fleet and Supreme Allied Commander Atlantic
1 May 1965	Retired from active duty

Authorization

The U.S. Naval Institute is hereby authorized to make available to libraries and other repositories of its choosing the transcripts of two oral history interviews concerning the life and career of Admiral Harold Page Smith. The two interviews were recorded on 12 July 1988 and 26 October 1990 in collaboration with Paul Stillwell for the U.S. Naval Institute.

The undersigned does hereby release and assign to the U.S. Naval Institute all right, title, restrictions, and interest in the interviews. The copyright in both the oral and transcribed versions shall be the sole property of the U.S. Naval Institute. The tape recordings of the interviews are and will remain the property of the U.S. Naval Institute.

Signed and sealed this 17th day of August 1991.

Admiral Harold Page Smith
U.S. Navy (Retired)

Interview Number 1 with Admiral Harold Page Smith, U.S. Navy (Retired)
Place: Admiral Smith's home in Virginia Beach, Virginia
Date: Tuesday, 12 July 1988
Interviewer: Paul Stillwell

Paul Stillwell: Admiral, it's a real delight to see you today and anticipate hearing your story commanding the USS *Missouri*.* How did you come to get such a prestigious job?

Admiral Smith: That is a long story. It happened in 1948—spring. My contemporaries were all getting cruisers, so I went over to Bureau of Personnel and said, "Where the hell is my cruiser?"

They said, "You already had your major command. You had a destroyer squadron in World War II."

I said, "That doesn't count. I need a cruiser now for selection purposes."

They said, all right, they'd give me a cruiser.

So as things wound up, I got *Missouri* instead of a cruiser.

Paul Stillwell: Well, I think it would also be interesting to interject the offer you had from Admiral Felix Johnson to be his chief of staff.†

Admiral Smith: Oh, yes, it was after I had—it must have been along about November or December of 1948 that I knew I was getting the *Missouri*. Admiral Felix Johnson, whom I'd known and visited with him down at his home on the Potomac, asked me if I would come and be his chief of staff in Commander Destroyers Atlantic Fleet. I told him that I could not; I had to get my major command while I could.

He said, "You serve me as a chief of staff, and I'll see that you get it."

---

* Captain Harold Page Smith, USN, commanded the USS *Missouri* (BB-63) from 5 February 1949 to 10 December 1949.
† Rear Admiral Felix L. Johnson, USN, commanded Destroyer Force Atlantic Fleet from 21 April 1948 to 25 August 1949. His oral history is in the Naval Institute collection.

I said, "My mother told me that when they pass the blueberry pie, you take the biggest piece, because it may not come around again. I've got to go take this ship."

Paul Stillwell: Was that considered the prize command for a surface captain at that time?

Admiral Smith: I think there's no doubt about it, no doubt about it.[*] Matter of fact, I didn't know anything about getting the *Missouri*. I was over in Paris when I got the news from Admiral Wooldridge, who wrote me and told me.[†] Apparently, they'd decided to give the *Missouri* to a captain who had never commanded a ship—a Naval Academy classmate of mine. Then they decided that wouldn't work, so they found one who'd commanded some ships.

Paul Stillwell: Who was the original nominee?

Admiral Smith: I've forgotten now. I don't know who it was, but I know it was a classmate.

Paul Stillwell: What kind of shape was the ship in when you took her over from Captain Thach?[‡]

Admiral Smith: She was not a clean or pretty ship for many, many reasons. The crew was small, nowhere near the proper complement for the ship. The worst feature, I think, was that the war color paint, which we had after World War II, was not a very lasting paint. So she wasn't pretty. They did the best they could, I suppose, but we simply had a lot of work to do trying to get her cleaned up. I got a few more men than Jimmy Thach had. I think my complement got up to around, maybe 1,600, 1,575, something like that.

---

[*] USS *Missouri* (BB-63) was commissioned 11 June 1944. She had a standard displacement of 45,000 tons and full-load displacement of 57,600 tons. She was 887 feet long and 108 feet in the beam. Her top speed was 33 knots. Initially she was armed with nine 16-inch guns, 20 5-inch guns, and 80 40-mm guns in quad mounts, and 49 20-mm guns in single mounts. She was best known as the site of the Japanese surrender in September 1945. At the time Smith took command she was the only active battleship in the U.S. Navy.
[†] Rear Admiral Edmund T. Wooldridge, USN, served in the Office of the Chief of Naval Operations, 1947-49.
[‡] Captain James H. Thach Jr., USN, commanded the *Missouri* from 24 February 1948 to 5 February 1949.

So I was able to—and I was a good first lieutenant too. I liked to walk the ship and see that the people did their jobs.

I found that her engineering department was in excellent shape; they were really splendid. I had been engineer officer myself of a cruiser, the *Marblehead*, earlier. I knew a little bit about it. Then I discovered that they were not carrying out below-decks inspections to the ultimate. So I entered on a program of inspecting every double-bottom cofferdam in the ship—some 300 or 400 of them. We found some of them that were loaded with World War II supplies, some that since the war end had never been opened. She wasn't a clean ship even when I turned her over to my relief, because we just simply did not have the paint that lasted.

Paul Stillwell: How well trained was the crew at that point?

Admiral Smith: I think well enough—quite good. George Peckham was executive officer.* A tough guy, a good sailor, not well liked, but execs aren't supposed to be well liked.

Paul Stillwell: That's his job.

Admiral Smith: That's his job to be tough and rough. But with Jimmy Thach's half of—more than half of the time—and my time, the *Missouri* was wearing the battle efficiency pennant when she ran aground.†

Paul Stillwell: How ironic.

Admiral Smith: Yes, she was. She beat all the other cruisers.

---

* Commander George E. Peckham, USN.
† The *Missouri* ran aground near Norfolk, Virginia, on 17 January 1950. She was not refloated until 1 February. See Dr. Malcolm Muir, Jr., "Hard Aground on Thimble Shoal," *Naval History*, Fall 1991, pages 30-35. The battle efficiency pennant is awarded annually to the top-performing ship in a category or group.

Paul Stillwell: Well, the wartime complement had probably been more than 2,500, so that was quite a contrast with . . .

Admiral Smith: Something like 2,700, 2,800—something like that, I think, in wartime.

Incidentally, getting the ship, Captain Dennison then was chief of staff to the President. He had me over to his house for cocktails, and President Truman was there.[*] President Truman obviously wanted to take a look at this guy to see if he was good enough to take his ship.

Paul Stillwell: Obviously you passed the test.

Admiral Smith: I passed inspection right where I was. Talked to him a few minutes. Truman was a very direct, straightforward kind of a man, very positive.

Paul Stillwell: Did you have any contacts with him during your time in command?

Admiral Smith: Never, no, nothing.

Paul Stillwell: He had visited the ship when Dennison was the captain, rode up from South America on board.

Admiral Smith: Yes, but he never visited while I was on that command.

Paul Stillwell: What do you remember of the change of command? You told me before the tape started it was rather a low-key affair.

---

[*] As a captain and rear admiral, Robert L. Dennison, USN, served as naval aide to President Harry S. Truman from February 1948 to January 1953. The oral history of Dennison, who retired as a four-star admiral, is in the Naval Institute collection. Truman was from the state of Missouri, and his daughter Margaret had christened the ship at the launching in 1944.

Admiral Smith: Yes, it was. I reported aboard and had lunch with the captain. Then we had the crew at quarters, and I inspected just the crew. Then he read his orders, and I read my orders and made a little speech and relieved him.

Paul Stillwell: Had you spent a period of a few days in a turnover with him?

Admiral Smith: No, not at all, just came down.

I was going to be on my toes about this big ship, because I'd never handled anything as big as that. I knew how to handle destroyers well enough; they were easy. And I knew the old battleships. I'd been on midshipman cruises in the *Kansas*, *North Dakota*, and *South Carolina*. And I'd been in the battleships *Idaho*, *Arizona*, and *Nevada*. And even the midshipman cruise, my first class cruise, I stood junior officer of the deck to keep station a little bit. Then I was always a watch officer in the other battleships. So I knew a slow, lumbering craft, but this thing was just like a destroyer, just big. Beautiful ship to handle.

Paul Stillwell: Did you take her out soon after you got command to become familiar?

Admiral Smith: Within a very few days I went to sea to meet a task force containing an aircraft carrier. I'll never forget—the carrier and destroyer were coming down from Newport. I came out of the harbor at Norfolk, out the channel, Thimble Shoals, and headed north, found the task force. I tried to head in around the end, and they'd turned toward me to launch aircraft. Then I tried to run down the other end, and they'd turn that way. So I headed right down the middle. I took the conn, of course, and as luck would have it, I put the rudder over to take the station, and it came up within a couple hundred yards of position.[*] So I turned to the officer of the deck and said, "Take the conn. Ship's in station." That started off well; I was a good sailor.

Paul Stillwell: Well, sometimes you need that kind of luck.

---

[*] The individual with the conn—normally an officer—directs the ship's movements in course and speed.

Admiral Smith: Yes.

Paul Stillwell: What do you remember about your officers of the deck?

Admiral Smith: I had a good bunch; they were all confident. I think Jimmy Thach had trained them well. They had a confidence when I first knew them, but later on, when I took the ship after the grounding, why, some of them lost that confidence. They were a little frightened. But after they realized I was a good ship handler—and I always told the watch officers wherever I was, "The worst mistake you can make is not to call me if there's any doubt. That's the worst mistake you can make—not to call me." Fortunately, I had some confidence, so that was easy.

Paul Stillwell: Did you wind up spending a fair amount of time in the sea cabin, staying close to the bridge?

Admiral Smith: In formations, yes; at sea, not too much. I didn't stay much in my in-port cabin, the big cabin. It's just too long a haul to get up there in case there was an emergency. Some awful silly people rode ships in these oceans back then.

I remember a Japanese ship coming right through our carrier task force formation. She was the burdened vessel; we had the right of way.* We all had to duck her.

Paul Stillwell: When was that?

Admiral Smith: That would have been in 1949.

Paul Stillwell: During one of the midshipman cruises?

Admiral Smith: No, it was one of the fleet exercises.

---

* Under the nautical rules of the road, the burdened ship has the obligation to avoid those with the right of way. In this case the ships with the right away maneuvered to avoid.

Paul Stillwell: Well, these battleships that you mentioned earlier were maybe 600 feet long, and this one is nearly 900 feet long. What adjustments did you have to make?

Admiral Smith: We just forget about the old ones; the old ones were just big tubs. It'd take forever to answer the rudder; it'd take forever to answer the few changes and few turns—changes in speed.* But the *Missouri* was so simple. I remember when I made my first fueling alongside a tanker with *Missouri*; I slipped in and matched her 12-knot speed or whatever it was. I found that just by one turn off, one turn on—I even got to where you could say, "I want, say, X-number of plus one-half." And she'd stick there, in calm weather.

But then, just a tiny little motion, and you could take off a turn, a tiny little motion and you could take off a turn, and she'd sit there. I do know that the crew had not always had that kind of luck, because on my first tour alongside a tanker, people in the forecastle I could see, and probably same there, had axes in their hands to cut the lines. Some captain had pulled the lines out, and they'd had to cut them. But we never had that kind of trouble.

Although *Caloosahatchee* once, one of the oilers—the captain was reading a book on his bridge, and I was perfectly calm on mine. All of a sudden, *Missouri* forged ahead, so I stopped and hollered at the tanker, "What happened?"

He hollered up, "The engine's lost power." Came back up. But we wavered back and forth a little bit, but did not pull a line. Didn't have to stop fueling.

Paul Stillwell: Did you ever have a concern when you were refueling destroyers that you might suck them in too close?

Admiral Smith: No, we knew what they should do, how they should handle themselves. Don't try to turn away too sharply and throw your stern into the ship. But if you fuel them forward, as you should, why, you wouldn't suck them in. I never had difficulty with a destroyer.

---

* In this case a "turn" refers to a revolution per minute of the propellers.

Paul Stillwell: How capable were the helmsmen that you had?

Admiral Smith: Excellent, just splendid. Splendid. And she was so easy to handle for a helmsman. Right rudder came over real quick, and the ship immediately turned, not like the old tubs, we called them—take forever to answer.

Paul Stillwell: One interesting feature of that class is that the rudders could operate independently. Did you ever have occasion to do that?

Admiral Smith: No, never did. Only found one interesting thing about the rudders. It happened once in Guantánamo Bay while riding to an ebb tide.* The maneuver area was rather small, and the water was shallow, and I couldn't turn her. I spent a few minutes to turn her, to head out. So I backed out, and I got a signal from the signal tower, "Is that the Weehawken Ferry?" [Laughter] Double-ended.

Paul Stillwell: Well, fairly soon after you took command, you had a couple of cruises with Naval Reservists. One went up north to New York City and up to Narragansett Bay, and one south to the Panama Canal Zone. Was that a regular mission of the ship in those days, to train reservists?

Admiral Smith: It had to be. There wasn't any other ship that could take the numbers of people that we did. I believe I took 900 midshipmen, and so we could take that number of reservists, without displacing any of the crew. Although midshipman cruises back in the '20s—the midshipmen displaced a lot of crew. They kept proper petty officers, of course, but we had to do the crew's work—passing coal, firemen firing the boilers. Dekey Simon out of my class and I took over firing two boilers; normally it took four firemen. Just he and I used to do it, just to make men of ourselves. Got pretty tired too.

Paul Stillwell: I'll bet.

---

* Guantanamo Bay, on the south coast of Cuba, near the eastern end of the island, for many years provided a fleet anchorage and training area for U.S. Navy ships.

Well, we've talked about how the crew was smaller than World War II. That explains how you had the room.

Admiral Smith: Yes. Had plenty of room.

Paul Stillwell: Did you have a special training program set up for these reservists?

Admiral Smith: Oh, yes, always a full schedule of drills they go through. They just simply joined the ship's company and did the regular drills with us. You did quite a lot of drills in the ships, of course. And we did, especially, because we did win the battle efficiency pennant.

Paul Stillwell: Did the reserve officers, who came along with them, in part run the training for them?

Admiral Smith: Oh, yes, yes. Let's say the unit joined a division. Their leader became the assistant division officer or deputy division officer. As a matter of fact, the division officer liked to have them run it.

Paul Stillwell: Well, that's good training for the reserve officers too.

Admiral Smith: Good training, good training.

Paul Stillwell: Do you remember any specific incidents from either the north cruise or the south cruise?

Admiral Smith: I simply do not. No, they all just went well off all right. I just don't remember anything about them, except that there was never a problem.

Paul Stillwell: When the ship would go places like New York or Newport or Panama, was there an outpouring of visitors to come aboard?

Admiral Smith: Yes, always. She was very popular. And here in Norfolk—now, you know, in Norfolk on any visiting day, there'll be two or three ships open. *Missouri* was open every day. We had visitors every day of the week. We'd run them off at 4:30 or 5:00 o'clock so the crew could eat.

Paul Stillwell: What do you remember about gunnery practice in the ship?

Admiral Smith: *Missouri*'s gunnery was perfectly splendid—16-inch battery, and the 5-inch guns as well. Excellent gunnery. I had splendid young gunnery officers too.

I remember one little event about the 16's. In a fleet exercise—Army, Navy, Air Force, Marines—at Vieques, Puerto Rico, the judges, the umpires for the exercise—the landing and the conflict, of course, ashore, opposed landing—some of the judges thought that the Marine judges were giving the *Missouri* too much capability for accuracy in gunfire. So they asked for a demonstration—*Missouri* 5,000 yards off the beach and hit the waterline with a 16-inch bullet. Well, it was amazing, the first bullet hit, kicked up just sand. The second bullet a tiny bit lower; the second bullet kicked up mostly water. And the third bullet kicked up water and sand. So they could hit the water line at 5,000 yards.

Paul Stillwell: Sounds like you got a solid, technical crew in the gunnery department.

Admiral Smith: They were very good.

There was a lieutenant—I'll never forget this one lieutenant, wartime, ex-temporary—Robbingham? Robbinghurst? I hadn't thought about it till just this moment. He was a splendid young man who was a great help to the gunnery officer and the assistant gunnery officer. Splendid. He was an assistant plotting room officer. But I'll never forget how good he was and what an excellent watch officer he was too. I don't know whether he stayed on in the Navy or not. I think he did not. I think he intended to go out and do something else with his life.

Paul Stillwell: What sorts of tactical formations were you in with the carriers when you operated with them?

Admiral Smith: Oh, it was just a couple thousand yards, one direction or another. Nothing very complicated.

Paul Stillwell: Was it the same plan, to provide antiaircraft protection, as had been during World War II?

Admiral Smith: That was part of it. They might put us in the quadrant where you might expect an enemy attack to come, but the enemy never does that, of course. They go where the concentration isn't the heaviest. Up in Iwo Jima I used to put my destroyers where the Japs came last time and put the little ships—PCs, whatever else—around the other side of the island.[*] The Japs always hit the PCs and left us destroyers alone.

Paul Stillwell: How capable was the antiaircraft battery against the jets that were coming in during that postwar period?

Admiral Smith: Fire control was very good. As a matter of fact, our Navy fire control systems were so superior to anything else that I knew about.

I'll give you just one little example. This departs from the *Missouri*, but when I had DesRon 4, I was told by Admiral Spruance to take my three best destroyers and escort the *Saratoga* out to the British Eastern Fleet.[†] After I got out there and cleaned boilers and other things, I asked the rear admiral of the destroyers if I couldn't have a target practice, that my ships hadn't fired at a target for some time. He said, "Well, yes, I'd like to go with you."

---

[*] Captain Smith commanded Destroyer Squadron Four from April 1944 to September 1945. PC – patrol craft.
[†] Admiral Raymond A. Spruance, USN, served as Commander Fifth Fleet during the Central Pacific campaign in 1944-45. The aircraft carrier *Saratoga* (CV-3) arrived in Ceylon on 31 March 1944 to operate with the British Far Eastern Fleet. See *Sara* in the East, *U.S. Naval Institute Proceedings*, December 1961, page 75.

Commodore Arliss, who was killed in Kenya later on, went with me on my first operation.* Then with the voice radio, I said, "Now *Dunlap* will fire first, one gun only. This is a director practice, not a gun practice." So here came a tow plane towing a target sleeve, and on the third shot, *Dunlap* shot it down.

Commodore Arliss said, "Please pick that up. I've never seen one shot down."

Our gunnery was far, far superior. It's a question of money. They didn't have the money, didn't have the ability to produce those things.

Paul Stillwell: I've seen a picture of you with Lord Mountbatten during that occasion.† He was out there at that time also.

Admiral Smith: Yes. I had a nice letter from him, thanking me from the service and so on out there.

I went up to Kandy in Ceylon. Of course, we put into Trincomalee, and I went up to call on Admiral Mountbatten. Then he came down, returned the call, inspected my three destroyers. He was very interested in our destroyers. He said, "Now, in *Kelly*, we had the torpedo director here. Much better, don't you think?"‡

"No, sir, much better where we've got it." But he talked like a destroyer man. I later became a very close friend of his in England. I was there three years with him as Chief Defence Staff when I was CinCUSNavEur.§ And he did so many nice things for us, and very fond of Dee and me both, I guess.**

The reason I got that picture signed the way it is—the picture you may have seen of Mountbatten with me out in Ceylon. After Dee got to know him, she had said to me, "What a handsome man."

---

* Captain Stephen H. T. Arliss, Royal Navy.
† Admiral Louis Mountbatten, Royal Navy, Supreme Allied Commander Southeast Asia, 1943-46.
‡ From 1939 to 1941 Captain Mountbatten commanded the 5th Destroyer Flotilla with HMS *Kelly* as his flagship.
§ As a four-star admiral, Smith served as Commander in Chief U.S. Naval Forces Eastern Atlantic and Mediterranean (CinCNELM), U.S. Commander Eastern Atlantic, and Commander in Chief U.S. Naval Forces Europe (CinCUSNavEur) from February 1960 to April 1963. Admiral of the Fleet Mountbatten served as Britain's Chief of Defence Staff from 1959 to 1965.
** Dee was the name of Admiral Smith's wife.

I said, "Well, hell, I'm better looking than Mountbatten; it's just that it was his photographer."

So he sent her this picture to prove that he's better looking than I am. [Laughter]

Paul Stillwell: When you got back from those two reserve cruises, you had a brief shipyard period at Norfolk of about three weeks. Do you recall anything specific accomplished then?

Admiral Smith: No, I do know that the shipyard was not overloaded at that time. A classmate of mine was Bob Swart, engineering duty.* He wasn't commanding the station, but he was commanding the overhaul facilities, and he gave me a splendid overhaul.

I remember only one funny thing. When we put in, I told the executive officer, "We will not have those sandwich vans out there on the dock at 5:00 o'clock. The ship puts out a perfectly excellent evening meal; I want the sailors to eat it."

The next day, here came three sandwich men, and one said, "Captain, for God's sake, we've been waiting for this ship. You're taking our livelihood; it's been a poor year." They went on, "And the sailors really like our sandwiches; they're good sandwiches. They're not expensive."

So I said, "Okay."

I don't remember very much about that overhaul except it was a good one. They kept the ship reasonably clean. I'd make them—at the end of the working day, don't leave the damn mess. And we policed the ship pretty much, and we came out fairly clean.

Paul Stillwell: Well, in your collateral duty as first lieutenant, did you generally upgrade the appearance of the ship?

Admiral Smith: We did; yes, I think we did.

---

* Captain Robert L. Swart, USN.

Paul Stillwell: Did you get some better paint?

Admiral Smith: No. We never did. We had to depend on painting just at the proper time. Don't ever paint if it's going to rain tomorrow. And watch it just as you do fertilizing your lawn, you know. Just pay attention to the weather is the only thing I could do. See that the surface was properly prepared as much as we could.

The first lieutenant was maybe not happy about my taking over a lot of his job; however, we got along fine.[*] Had no problem with officers, nor they with me.

Paul Stillwell: You still had the catapults and the floatplanes at that point. How were they used?

Admiral Smith: Just the old business of occasionally we had the opportunity to fire them off for training. And yet, you had, really, to do an awful lot of maneuvering to give the catapult directly into the wind shot. You had to turn 90 degrees away from the wind so that the bulk of the ship didn't cause an eddy and create confusion with the catapult.

Paul Stillwell: And then you had to create a slick for them to land on.

Admiral Smith: That's easy. You'd make a big slick.

Paul Stillwell: So launching was the harder task.

Admiral Smith: Yes, yes, that was.

Paul Stillwell: Well, at least in a ship like that you wouldn't have a roll to contend with also.

---

[*] In a Navy ship it is the job of the first lieutenant to oversee the preservation and cleanliness of the ship.

Admiral Smith: No. Some guy said once, "You call this sea duty? The ship don't even move." At 38-foot depth, why, she didn't. It took a pretty good sea to make her move any.

Paul Stillwell: Were those planes used very much?

Admiral Smith: Pretty much, yes. They had to get their regular hours in. We flew them off sometimes just to fly, get in some hours and training. But I think they got more training on the midshipman cruises than at any other time.

    I remember one interesting feature, though. Admiral Smith would always work up a war game with the destroyers seeking the *Missouri*.* We had one going over on the first cruise, and I won it. We had another one coming back, and I won that one. When they started talking about a war game, tactical game, on the way to Cherbourg, I said, "Admiral, well, hell, I win all those things."

    He said, "No, you wait till you see what I'm going to do to you this time." They put me down where I lost speed, lost engines for ten minutes, or something like that. But I never lost to the destroyers. I knew what they had to do.

Paul Stillwell: Well, how did you manage to win?

Admiral Smith: Oh, always be where they weren't and missing their torpedoes and just guessing—a little bit of feel for it. I'd been a destroyer squadron commander myself, so I knew how to defend against them.

    It's not easy to tell about it. You have to take a half hour or [unclear] to describe one of those, I guess.

Paul Stillwell: Well, part of it's almost instinct too.

---

* Rear Admiral Allan E. Smith, USN, Commander Cruiser Force Atlantic Fleet.

Admiral Smith: It is instinct, of course it is—a feel. And it's a feel for handling your ship, really. You know approximately what the ship does, how much she slows—one knot for 100 yards and so on. But there can be differences in the weather.

Paul Stillwell: There was some fog to contend with on the first midshipman cruise. How did you handle that?

Admiral Smith: Well, with the radar that we had, there was no problem, ever, I don't think. We did slow, because you never know what merchant ship you might blunder into, and he can't see, maybe. So you have to duck him. So we obeyed the rules of the road pretty well, laws of the sea.

Paul Stillwell: Well, just looking at the ship's log, it was a very leisurely transit across the Atlantic. How did you spend the time?

Admiral Smith: Again, drill, drill, drill. The cruises in my midshipman days, of course, it was just the school of the ship is the school of the sailor. You didn't need any of this nonsense of book learning. But with the midshipmen cruises that I took in 1949, quite a lot of study periods, a lot of lectures and work like that, as well as the ship's work, and midshipmen standing watches.

Paul Stillwell: Was that training pretty well administered by people from the academy?

Admiral Smith: Very well, very well.

Paul Stillwell: How much did the crew itself have to contribute to that?

Admiral Smith: I think quite a lot. I think the crew—my petty officers, especially—had to be very good working with the—[looking for pictures] it's in there, I guess; there's a picture of Smedberg and Count Austin.* Did you see that one in there?

Paul Stillwell: I don't believe so.

Admiral Smith: Well, you go ahead, and I'll see if I can find it. Over in London.

Paul Stillwell: What was Smedberg on board for?

Admiral Smith: He had one of the jobs at the Naval Academy. Maybe one of those is plastered in here then. Oh, here we are. I had one of the squadron commander, destroyers, myself, Smedberg, and Austin, Mendenhall.†

Paul Stillwell: You all look very happy.

Admiral Smith: Yes. I told Dee that I was a better-looking guy than Mountbatten. [Laughter]

Paul Stillwell: It's in the eye of the beholder.

Admiral Smith: Oh, me. Wonderful man.

Paul Stillwell: What do you remember about the reception in England when the ship got there?

Admiral Smith: I do recall the English came in great crowds, and we did all we could to see that they saw as much of the ship as they could at the time. We had to run the routes,

---

* Captain William R. Smedberg III, USN; he was then head of the electrical engineering department at the Naval Academy. Captain Bernard L. Austin, USN. The oral histories of the two, both of whom retired as vice admirals, are in the Naval Institute collection.
† Captain William K. Mendenhall Jr., USN.

really, so they wouldn't get fouled up, and move right along. But I know they enjoyed it. The English just love ships. They invented the things, they think.

Paul Stillwell: I wish you'd please repeat that story about the lady that came to make a presentation to you.

Admiral Smith: Oh, yes.

We'd just gotten in and gotten through the ceremonies receiving the commander in chief of the British Atlantic Fleet—Admiral of Fleet Sir Algernon Willis.[*] He came aboard and had his 19 guns. The first question he asked me was, "Captain, how do you like your moorings?"

I said, "Admiral, they're splendid."

He said, "They damn well should be; they cost me a lot of money."

But then I got out of that, went on up to my cabin to start reading the mail that just arrived from Washington. A Marine orderly came in and said, "A lady wants to see you."

I said, "Ask her to see the watch duty officer or the executive officer."

He said, "She has to see you."

So the little lady came in, and she was carrying a tiny plate—obviously her prize possession. She made a little speech that she wanted to give me this plate as an expression of thanks from the English people to the American people through me for all we did for them in World War II. And I still have that plate right in there, in the locker. I sat her down and gave her a cup of tea, and we talked about England for a bit. She went on her way. I wrote her a letter.

But they were very happy to see us. England was still on short rations. They were still in straitened circumstances, I'd say.

Paul Stillwell: You told me earlier that the visitors cleaned out the larder when you put out a buffet for them.

---

[*] The *Missouri* moored at Portsmouth, England, from 17 to 25 June 1949.

Admiral Smith: When we had a reception with hams and beefs and cheeses and things, why, they ate them all; they ate everything. They were hungry. God knows they'd been through a lot of torment—the German bombings.

Paul Stillwell: It would be helpful if you'd explain a little more about the background on Sir Algernon Willis and why the moorings were so expensive.

Admiral Smith: Oh, I was told by dispatch from London that I would go alongside the south railway jetty in Portsmouth. So I asked for a chart and found out that the south right-of-way jetty had water of something like 28 feet alongside, and the *Missouri* drew 38. So I told them by dispatch, I told London that I would anchor out in the Spithead. And, of course, they didn't want that at all; they wanted her in. So they did a lot of dredging and they put sponsons out from the jetty so as to give *Missouri* enough water under her keel.

Paul Stillwell: And that obviously facilitated the visiting by the English.

Admiral Smith: Oh, very much, very much. They couldn't possibly have handled it if I'd been out at Spithead.

Paul Stillwell: How much touring and visiting did the Americans do in England?

Admiral Smith: Our sailors and the midshipmen had four days each watch in London, or wherever they wanted to go, and they took it. I never got out of Portsmouth; I couldn't make the trip myself.

Paul Stillwell: Was that because of a heavy social schedule?

Admiral Smith: Yes, it was, it was. I think the nicest of the social events—they were many, but on a Sunday in port, Admiral Willis asked me to luncheon with him and Lady Willis at their quarters. He showed me two pigs he was raising, and he showed me his garden—the vegetables he was raising—but he was really splendid old Scot. And we got along fine. He never asked Hokey Smith even.[*]

Paul Stillwell: Why would you think that was?

Admiral Smith: Just didn't take to him.

Paul Stillwell: What kind of an embarked admiral was Admiral Smith?

Admiral Smith: All right, as far as I'm concerned. I really never did have a problem. I really was lucky enough to know how to handle the ship, and so he never had any fault or complaint with my handling.

I do remember once Captain Mendenhall had tried by signal to maneuver the destroyers and the *Missouri* to a fueling station. And it didn't go off well, so Admiral Smith canceled it and told the ships to proceed independently to their fueling, and so I headed around and up to the port side of the *Caloosahatchee*, I guess it was.

Someone told me later that Admiral Smith said to the guests—all the Naval Academy people and civilian colleges, NROTC college professors down at his flag bridge—said, "Just watch this; this is going to be perfect."[†] And, sure enough, just as luck would have it, I slid alongside, stopped, got over the lines, never moved an inch.

Paul Stillwell: Well, since he had that kind of confidence in you, you had it made.

Admiral Smith: He had the confidence, yes. So I'm damn sure he'd have been rough if I'd had some bad luck or some bad judgment, or whatever.

Paul Stillwell: How much of the social part of it did he handle during the cruises?

Admiral Smith: He had his own and I had mine; we never went to the same places.

---

[*] Allan Smith's nickname was Hoke.
[†] NROTC – Naval Reserve Officers' Training Corps, a program that provides training leading to officer commissions at selected universities.

Paul Stillwell: Who arranged that? Was that the attaché's office or CinCNELM?

Admiral Smith: For what we did, CinCNELM would help out, but what the British did, why, they managed. We got in. Except for what we did aboard ship, the British issued invitations to various kinds of things we went to. And when the midshipmen and the crew went to London, why, they were pretty much on their own. Very little shore patrol, some.

Paul Stillwell: Were there any special arrangements, like package tours or what have you, for the sailors?

Admiral Smith: No, not in those days.

Paul Stillwell: I know they did have that sort of thing in the '50s; American Express ran it.

Admiral Smith: I don't remember any package tours. I suppose they could have got them, but I don't think anything was arranged for them. Take the nearest train to London is the best way to do it.

Paul Stillwell: Do you recall Admiral Fraser, Lord Fraser, visiting?[*]

Admiral Smith: Yes, yes, I remember giving him a little memento, a chunk of the *Missouri* deck and a little replica of the surrender plaque. And he said he always wanted a piece of the American Navy. I had him to lunch and gave him this little souvenir.

Paul Stillwell: Well, he had been on hand for the surrender, so that was certainly appropriate.

---

[*] Admiral Sir Bruce Fraser, Royal Navy, had been Commander in Chief British Pacific Fleet during World War II. On 2 September 1945 he was on board the *Missouri* to sign the surrender documents on behalf of Great Britain.

Admiral Smith: Yes, yes. He said he wanted a piece of it.

He was a man with a great deal of charm and energy and wit. I liked him; I liked him first rate. I saw him again when he was getting to be quite an old man. I saw him at some reception in 1960-61, along in that era. I was in London '60-63.

Paul Stillwell: I think he lived till the 1970s.[*]

Admiral Smith: Yes, but he did not get out a lot of the—just like I do, I go to very few of the active Navy deals. I've had enough retired naval officers down here for me to see.

Paul Stillwell: Were there any other expressions of gratitude from the British people, besides the one lady you mentioned?

Admiral Smith: Oh, I think they were very kindly disposed to us, of course, saying nice things about them, about the ship. She didn't look as pretty as I'd like because of the war color just wouldn't stick like it should. It's better now. I don't know what their formula is today for the war paint that won't burn.

But the old war color burned badly in World War II.

Paul Stillwell: What do you remember about the use of helicopters during those midshipman cruises?[†]

Admiral Smith: Of course, the floatplanes did some work, but the helicopters delivered mail every morning. Aboard *Missouri*, we put out a daily news sheet and we delivered a packet of them to each of the nine destroyers every morning.

Paul Stillwell: Was this helicopter operating from the turret top?

---

[*] Fraser was born 5 February 1888 and died 12 February 1981 at age 93.
[†] The Sikorsky HO3S was a two-rotor helicopter that first entered Navy service in 1946. The main rotor diameter was 49 feet, length of the aircraft 45 feet, gross weight, 5,500 pounds; maximum speed, 103 miles per hour.

Admiral Smith: Yes, yes.

Paul Stillwell: I suppose with the catapults back there and the crane, it was too crowded on the fantail.

Admiral Smith: It was, yes.

I remember only one episode of—again, we used to have to make about a 90-degree turn to give the helicopter proper wind direction and no eddy currents.

I remember once, right off here, I had some one of our cruises, reserve cruises or whatever. I had a couple helicopters, and as I was going to release them to go back to Norfolk, they were commanded to report to an aircraft carrier in company, in the same formation. And the senior helicopter pilot asked me, "For God's sake, don't send me to that carrier. They just do not take care of helicopters." And within a few hours he was dead. I'll never forget that; I don't remember his name.

But those helicopters are very delicate birds. You've got to give them plenty of good attention, and we always did. We never had any difficulty with any of them.

Paul Stillwell: Are there any special memories you have of the second cruise, the one that went to France?

Admiral Smith: The second cruise was interesting in one way. I had three black gentlemen, guests of the Secretary of Defense. And I was concerned a bit. I thought that it might present difficulties, but it did not. That was the one interesting event of the cruise. They were all fairly good.

I remember that one of the black guests was what we would call the Drew Pearson of the *Chicago Defender*.* I'll never forget the name of the newspaper. And he was supposed to be a tough one. But I saw the wonderful side of him when, just out of Cherbourg, it happened that one of the messmen was on report by the shore patrol for fighting with the shore patrol. And the offense was fairly grave, because he had drawn a

---

* Andrew Pearson was a muckraking syndicated newspaper columnist. The *Chicago Defender* was a prominent black paper of the era.

knife. So he got knocked out, of course, with a billy club and on report. And he was intoxicated. He wasn't really responsible for what he was doing.

But at mast the next morning, I gave him a summary court-martial.* And Admiral Smith said, "You must get the three black gentlemen in and tell them what happened."

I said, "Admiral, they know, they know. I don't have to tell them. They'll think it's odd that I call them in."

He said, "Tell them."

So I asked them up—cup of coffee—and I said, "Now, look, I just want to tell you about something that happened last night in Cherbourg and something I had to do this morning."

After I'd finished my story, why, the *Chicago Defender* man—the Drew Pearson we were afraid of—said, "Look, captain, you didn't have to tell us that. We've been on this ship long enough to know this ship gives the black man a fair deal. If the messman drew the knife, he deserved a court-martial." So I think we did a good job with them anyway.

The only problem with Cherbourg, I recall, was that it was rather tiny, tiny port. Again, I told them that there was only one berth in the harbor where I could anchor and sweep to anchor. And that was where the Queens came in to drop their anchor.† So they gave me that berth. And I'll never forget the pilot. I had to take the French pilot in through the gate and into the harbor. And he headed me for the mooring—[Unclear] Point—and he said, "Now, captain, we've placed a buoy where we feel is the center of the—" He said, "Now you take your ship—you know how to handle your ship; you take your ship and drop your anchor."

So my navigator was working all the time, anyway. And when he said let go, we dropped the anchor on the buoy. You wouldn't believe it. Dropped the anchor on the buoy.

---

* Captain's mast is a sort of court in which the commanding officer of a unit listens to requests, awards non-judicial punishment, or issues commendations. Most often captain's mast is used for punishment of lesser offenses than those that merit courts-martial

† This refers to the *Queen Mary* and *Queen Elizabeth*, two prominent British ocean liners of the era.

But we swung to anchor, and each one of the Queens came in during the time we were there. Each one of them would anchor to the west of us and be held by tugs so that she wouldn't swing into us with tide.

Paul Stillwell: That's an expensive way to prevent a collision. Was it possible to go alongside then at Cherbourg?

Admiral Smith: No. No, they had no pier there, it was . . .

Paul Stillwell: I guess it came along a few years later, because by the early '50s, they could.

Admiral Smith: They couldn't at my time, no.

But they had tugs and ferries of sorts that would come on. They had a good, big ferry would bring out guests. We had a lot of guests from the French. Not the same kind of interest, I guess, as the British. But quite a lot; they came out.

Paul Stillwell: And they didn't eat all your ham and roast beefs.

Admiral Smith: No, they were better fed. They had farmers that still had plenty of pigs to eat, I guess. No, they did not have the same appetites the British had.

Paul Stillwell: You mentioned these black visitors had observed that the Negro sailors—to use the term of that period—were treated fairly. Was that something that the command fostered, or how did that come about?

Admiral Smith: Oh, yes. Yes, we did. We very definitely did. I remember that I'd only been aboard a short time when we were going to have port and starboard receptions. And the executive officer, to test me, he said, "Now, will there be a separate party for the stewards and the black sailors?"

"No, sir," I said, "port and starboard watch. We'll have two parties." And my wife and I went to both of them.

Paul Stillwell: What about, in doing their jobs or having berthing assignments or so forth, were they just the same treatment as whites?

Admiral Smith: Same as white men, yes. As far as I ever knew, there was absolutely no discrimination in that ship. Not a bit. And there was never a fight, except that unfortunate case in Cherbourg, where the intoxicated boy wanted to fight.

Paul Stillwell: You mentioned before we started the tape, also, about the black helmsman. I think that would be an interesting story.

Admiral Smith: Oh, yes.

On my first few hours out of Norfolk, the three guests came with the guide, came up the bridge. And just by the darnedest chance—I think of my eight helmsmen, there was only one black sailor, and he just had the watch. He was there. And I think, at least one of the reporters thought that this was a put-up job, so he went up to the helmsman and whispered something to him. And the helmsman shouted, "I've been on this watch for seven months."

Paul Stillwell: So he was a credible witness.

Admiral Smith: He was a credible witness.

Paul Stillwell: What are the satisfactions and pleasures that come to a captain in commanding a ship like that?

Admiral Smith: Oh, you've got the biggest, the finest, the best there is in the world—the fastest and the smoothest. I remember an admiral told my wife when he knew about my getting the command, he said, "Now, honey, you're going to be number two for another year." That's about right. You really love the thing; that's what you live for.

I'll never forget that the senior team Navy captain on the Joint War Plans Committee I told you about, he said, "You know, I had four ambitions. I wanted to enter the Naval Academy; I wanted to graduate; I wanted to command a battleship; I wanted to be a flag officer." He said, "Well, I got the first three."

Paul Stillwell: So he was an aviator?

Admiral Smith: No, he was surface, surface officer. He didn't make flag rank.

Paul Stillwell: Well, I've talked to a number of men who made flag rank, and the preponderance of them look back and say that probably the command of a big ship was the highlight of a career.

Admiral Smith: Oh, it was more fun, I think. No, when you get on a more responsible job, I think you remember the interesting things that happened in your time.

Paul Stillwell: Well, it's a more tangible kind of satisfaction.

Admiral Smith: That's yours; you can run every inch of it.

See, when I took command the second time after the grounding for those next three months, another kind of interest. I knew I could handle the ship, and I wanted to show her off. I wanted to grandstand, and I did just that—flathat, those sailors called it. I had to reload the ship; I had to try to clean her up. As soon as she was loaded, we went to sea, and I was given three days of training time at Guantánamo—three days. Normally, when a ship has come out of a shipyard, as she had, why, you give her seven weeks of shakedown. I had three days, and the time was so short, I wouldn't let the training command come aboard. We trained our crew ourselves for three days.

Then we joined the joint maneuvers at Vieques again. This time, after I got over to Vieques, why, a whole planeload of Washington seniors came aboard, ten senators and

20-odd representatives. One of the senators was Harry Byrd Sr.—the old man.* I'll never forget something that's so interesting. The last act of the invasion was a six-gun salvo from the *Missouri*. And, that was in the cards, of course; everybody knew it. The senators and all the visitors were up on the—up above my bridge. And one of the senators, I remember, we worried about him because he had a bad heart. I thought that six guns can shake you. Really does. So as soon as the salvo was fired, I went up on the deck above. And they were all laughing, carrying on. Everybody was all right. And after we'd exchanged some pleasantries, why, Senator Byrd came up alongside of me, and he said, "Captain, how much does one of those rounds cost?"

I said, "Senator, just about the same as a Chevrolet automobile." That's when they cost $2,500 to $3,000.

Paul Stillwell: In what way were you grandstanding during that period?

Admiral Smith: Show off—if you proceed, better go at 25 knots and then slip right into station as smartly as you could. Don't creep in.

One grandstanding I did was right off Virginia Beach here coming back. There were people along the beach. It was too cold then for swimming, but there were people there. So I came in as close as possible, just let them see, maybe I'm going aground again. Just let them see the ship.

But down at Vieques, I remember that two vice admirals were going to go back to Washington with me. It was very rough, the south coast of Vieques, had an easterly sea and pretty rough. It would have been difficult to get room to put step onto the gangway.† So I had the executive officer down the gangway. I got the *Missouri* under way, and as the boat came past my bow, I whipped—kicked her ahead and made a hell of a big lee—I made a big wash there, got them aboard, then she was being swept down. I had to go through some other ships. So I kicked her to standard then. A lot of officers were on the bridge, too, to watch all of this. And I was very pleased to hear one young ensign say, "I

---

* Harry F. Byrd, a Democrat from Virginia, served in the Senate from 4 March 1933 until his resignation on 10 November 1965.
† The term "gangway" here refers to an accommodation ladder, a set of wooden stairs parallel to the side of the ship at approximately a 45-degree angle. It has a wooden platform at the bottom onto which a person can come aboard from a boat alongside.

hope some day I'll handle a destroyer as well as that." That pleased the old man, of course.

Paul Stillwell: Was this grandstanding deliberately to restore confidence?

Admiral Smith: Yes, yes. Yes, I did it deliberately.
And I loved every bit of it.

Paul Stillwell: How was the confidence of the crew in general when you came back?

Admiral Smith: Pretty bad, actually. They were shocked and shaken by the grounding. They hadn't expected that kind of thing ever to happen to them.

I remember that when I took command it was an odd thing.[*] It was sunset or after sunset, I guess. I got over to the post at the Navy yard and handed my orders to the officer of the deck and said, "Pass the word that Captain H. P. Smith has resumed command." And from all over the ship, you heard a cheer. In other words, that's something old-fashioned that's coming back, anyway.

Paul Stillwell: That also would make you feel good.

Admiral Smith: Yes.

Paul Stillwell: Did you have any contact with Captain Brown in that period?[†]

Admiral Smith: Only to tell him that I was taking command.

I was sitting at lunch on board the flagship with Admiral Wooldridge when the

---

[*] Commander George E. Peckham, USN, the executive officer, became acting commanding officer when Captain Brown was relieved on 3 February 1950. Captain Smith commanded the ship from 7 February 1950 to 19 April 1950.
[†] Captain William D. Brown, USN, commanded the USS *Missouri* (BB-63) from 10 December 1949 to 3 February 1950.

telephone rang and the steward said, "Admiral, for you."*

So Wooldridge said, "Yes, sir; yes, sir. Yes, sir—but, sir. Well, yes, sir. Aye, aye, sir." He hung up the phone, and he said, "Get packed, Smith. Get down to Norfolk."

I said, "Admiral, this is entirely wrong to send me, of all people, back down there. The Navy should know that any captain can take that ship. He should be prepared to do it and love it. I think it's wrong." However, when I got down there, I began to realize it was right.

But, at any rate, I got down and Admiral Smith gave me my orders, and it said, "Take temporary command of *Missouri*."†

I said, "Temporary? What does this mean?"

He said, "Well, you're going to be there a short time."

"Temporary," I said, "well, temporary command. Is Brown still in command?"

He said, "Yes."

I said, "Detach him. I will not go aboard if he's still captain." So I waited in his office for an hour or so while he got Admiral Fechteler to sign a new set of orders to take command.‡ And a set orders also detaching Captain Brown. You see, Captain Brown had a tremendous lot of friends. He was a splendid person. He'd been second-team all-American end on the Naval Academy football team. Very good. Had a fine war record. I never served with him during the war, but he certainly had a fine record. And many of his friends wanted to fight this case. Well, there wasn't any way in the world they could fight it. The best precept of that kind of a situation is what happened to the captain of the—I forget the name of the cruiser, one of the light cruisers, that ran aground in Crooked Island Passage.

Paul Stillwell: It was the *Omaha*.

---

* Rear Admiral Edmund T. Wooldridge, USN, commanded Destroyer Force Atlantic Fleet from 25 August 1949 to 27 July 1950. The flagship, a destroyer tender, was at Newport, Rhode Island.
† Rear Admiral Allan E. Smith, USN, Commander Cruisers Atlantic Fleet.
‡ Admiral William M. Fechteler, USN, had just taken over as Commander in Chief Atlantic Fleet on 1 February 1950.

Admiral Smith: *Omaha*.* And the skipper had—the officer of the deck and the navigator said, "Captain, you're too close."

He said, "No, plenty of room; I'll take it. I'll take the conn back."

So came time for court-martial, he said, "Look, there's no excuse for a court-martial. I'm entirely at fault; nobody else is at fault. It's all my fault. Goodbye."

Paul Stillwell: That obviously wasn't Captain Brown's reaction.

Admiral Smith: No, his friends were advising him not to—admirals.

Paul Stillwell: Was there some kind of arrangement envisioned where you would both be in some sort of command?

Admiral Smith: I don't know what they had in mind, but I would have no part of that.

Paul Stillwell: Well, you said your first reaction was that it was not a good idea for you to return. Why did you come to a different conclusion?

Admiral Smith: Well, that was after I saw that there were a lot of uncertainties in this ship's company. A lot of uncertainty in the officers of the deck, who should be perfectly confident but didn't have that confidence.

So, again, I had to tell them, "Look, the only mistake you make is don't call me now. If you don't call me and something happens, that's your worst mistake. You didn't call me." And they called me. I shouldn't confess this to your tape, but when I came back from the Vieques exercises I was on that bridge an awful lot sitting up, whatever. I got sacroiliac. And then I got the pain down the leg, the nerve, the sciatic nerve. Two of the guests on board, two charming gentleman, were surgeons from Mayos.† So I asked them, "What do I do?"

---

* The light cruiser *Omaha* (CL-4) went aground near Castle Island Light in the Bahamas on 19 July 1937. She was refloated on 29 July through the combined efforts of tugs, beach gear, and artificial waves from five destroyers. Captain Howard B. Mecleary, USN, commanded the *Omaha* from 1936 to 1938.
† The Mayo Clinic in Rochester, Minnesota, is highly regarded for its medical excellence.

"Oh, you've got to lay down flat. You've got to stay in bed."

No way. So they didn't have any help. But as soon as I got the ship back up here to Norfolk, I went over to Portsmouth Naval Hospital. I got to the bone man, who was a young man, lieutenant, and he took some pictures and pressed and punched. He said, "Captain, there's nothing wrong with you except you let your belly hang out. You've got to straighten that up."

I lay down and, "That hurts."

He said, "Yeah, it's going to hurt." But exercise is what is really needed." If I'd done exercises all the time, if I'd held myself a little more erect when I was tired, it wouldn't have happened. I know that now.

Paul Stillwell: That's tough to do when you've got all those demands of command.

Admiral Smith: And you're tired. That's when you let your belly hang out, as the lieutenant said.

Paul Stillwell: What kind of demands on stamina does that kind of a ship make?

Admiral Smith: Quite a lot, quite a lot. You have to be pretty well, pretty strong. I'd been through a lot of those things in World War II. Even after that I was strong enough to do things.

I remember one instance I took President Roosevelt aboard one of my destroyers at Juneau, Alaska.* I took him down through the Inland Passage in Canada. And down through Seymour Narrows with the big Ripple Rock in the middle of it and a 90-degree turn. And the tide goes through there at 17 knots each way—rain and fog.

Well, one of the admirals called me from the ship that I had the President in. The *Dunlap* was leading, and I had the *Cummings*. I had the President on board, with three doctors. And the admiral said, "What are your plans for tonight?"

---

* President Franklin D. Roosevelt went aboard the destroyer *Cummings* (DD-365) on 8 August 1944 for transportation to Seattle. She was part of Smith's Destroyer Squadron Four. On 12 August the President made a nationwide radio address from the deck of the *Cummings* while at the Puget Sound Navy Yard in Bremerton. For details see *Jim Bishop, FDR's Last Year: April 1944-April 1945* (New York: William Morrow & Company, 1974).

I said, "I'm going through Seymour Narrows if I can see. If I can't see, I'm going to anchor and wait till morning." I was going to pass through at midnight.

He said, "Well, the passenger has a date at 4:00 o'clock in Seattle."

I said, "I can get him there if we go outside Vancouver Island. The ships can take it. It's rough."

He said, "What's the weather?"

I said, "It's rough out there."

He said, "Well, the passenger can't take it."

So, as luck would have it, I crept into the entrance to Seymour Narrows at five knots; I was a little ahead of time. And the fog lifted, the rain stopped, I whipped on around Ripple Rock, and there were big eddies in there even so, even though it was low water, slack. Went through there, just got through, down came the fog, down came the rain.

Paul Stillwell: Somebody upstairs was helping you.

Admiral Smith: I was three days on that bridge in that stretch. So I could handle the *Missouri*.

Paul Stillwell: Wasn't that the occasion when the Republicans were squawking that the ship was sent to pick up the President's dog?

Admiral Smith: Yes, a damn lie. The President's dog was right on board with him. The sailors were getting it fat too, feeding him every chance they got. Fala was the name of the dog.

Paul Stillwell: And Roosevelt had that wonderful retort. He said, "I don't mind when they attack me and my wife and my children."

Admiral Smith: ". . . but not my dog."

Roosevelt had a nice sense of humor.

His family met him—his daughter and one or two of his sons.

Paul Stillwell: And I think you mentioned before the tape started that you had stayed up that whole night before going into England on the midshipman cruise.

Admiral Smith: Oh, yes. That was rather stormy, windy, rainy, and you enter—it's rather difficult water going into Spithead. And then had to turn the ship to anchor, because there's a hell of a fast current through there. So you were really on your toes.

And there's an awful lot of traffic, of course, in the English Channel. I remember when we passed Plymouth they were sailing a yacht race from Plymouth across to France. And at that stage of the game—in the late afternoon or early evening—it was fairly calm, but here comes the sailing ships in all directions. So I stopped, turned on the stoplights, just stopped. And two or three of these yachts bumped into the *Missouri*. I didn't hit them; they hit me. I just stopped and waited until they were all gone.

Paul Stillwell: Well, I've heard an interesting analogy in politics. That the reason the senators and so forth are able to carry on filibusters is that they've been through this long, arduous campaigning, so it's a natural selection process that you've got politicians who have stamina. I think probably the guy who rises to command of a major combatant has proven those qualities in other ships.

Admiral Smith: He's been away before, yes.

Paul Stillwell: Was Commander Peckham in any way scarred by the grounding?

Admiral Smith: Yes. Of course, he was scarred, just by association.

One odd thing happened. When I got back in after the cruise to the south, I had a letter addressed to me for Peckham from Admiral Smith, stating his intention to give him a letter of reprimand. And Peckham had been newly married just before I left the ship the first time. He was married in December, and I remember on that occasion we broke out all the *Missouri* silver, and I had 14 guests. And I had the Marine orderlies count the silver before anybody was allowed to leave. Didn't want President Truman to get me on that one. But I let Peckham go on home, and the next day I got ahold of him and said, "Now look, George, this is going to stick you. But there's nothing you can do about it. You can write till doomsday, but I'm the guy that writes the letter that tells them that you're no way responsible for this thing—which I will do."

Peckham was really shocked, and he did go to Washington, wrote his own letter and so on. But I reminded Admiral Smith, I said, "Remember now that this ship was wearing the battle efficiency pennant when she went aground. Remember also that Peckham was on the navigating bridge screaming to shift control to the bridge." And, of course, central station wouldn't do it unless the captain ordered it. Peckham did everything possible he could. And none of this touched him. Well, he withdrew the letter. I gave Peckham a splendid fitness report, but it was too late. And several other officers were touched as well.

Paul Stillwell: We've talked about good luck. That was a case of bad luck.

Admiral Smith: Bad luck.

Paul Stillwell: How was the length of that second command tour determined?

Admiral Smith: I suppose that they considered the ship had been brought back to reasonable standard, and then they had selected a captain—another classmate, Irving Duke—to come relieve me.[*] He'd been about halfway through a cruiser command, so he had had recent experience—immediate experience—of handling a major ship. So I suppose they thought it was all right. I'd done my job, whatever it was.

Paul Stillwell: It was during that Louis Johnson era of parsimony on budgets that the crew was cut back even further.[†] Did that affect you at all?

---

[*] Captain Irving T. Duke, USN, commanded the *Missouri* from 19 April 1950 to 2 March 1951.
[†] Louis A. Johnson served as Secretary of Defense from April 1949 until September 1950. He cut back substantially on defense expenditures, a program that had to be reversed with the beginning of the Korean War in June 1950. He was removed as SecDef a few months after the war started.

Admiral Smith: I remember when I got back in, one of my first fights was to keep from cutting the crew. They wanted to cut her down to 1,000.

Paul Stillwell: And make her a training ship.

Admiral Smith: And make her a training ship. Of course, I wrote on this subject, and my principal argument was, "Look, I need 1,500 men to get the ship out through the channel. She can't be a training ship with less than 1,500 people." And I went through another study, I think I came out 1,551 or some such odd number—each department, each division, exactly why we needed that many. We made quite a study of it. And she should have that number; you can't do with less and make any kind of a ship out of her.

Paul Stillwell: So your justification was successful.

Admiral Smith: Yes, but then I won the battle, whatever it was.

Paul Stillwell: Well, then the Korean War came along a few months later and really turned things around.*

Admiral Smith: Yes, Duke took her out to Korea. I remember he had something I never had; I never had really rough weather in the ship. And he, going past Hatteras, had some very rough weather. I think something broke loose on him, something not properly stored.

Paul Stillwell: What are your recollections of handling the ship in the roughest weather you did encounter?

---

* The Korean War began on 25 June 1950, when six North Korean infantry division and three border constabulary brigades invaded South Korea. The troops were supported by approximately 100 Russian-made T-34 tanks. In New York that same day the United Nations Security Council adopted a resolution condemning the invasion.

Admiral Smith: No problem. She is just so big that she didn't budge. You might slow her a little bit, a slower turn if she's turning into the wind, whatever, but no problem. Nothing.

Paul Stillwell: Did you feel any effect from those skegs near the propellers when you were trying to twist the ship?

Admiral Smith: I don't remember—no, I don't think so. She needed water under her keel. You could not turn her easily unless in dead-still water. But as I mentioned, trying to turn her to get out of Guantánamo Bay, I couldn't turn her around without sticking her nose in the mud. So I backed up.

Paul Stillwell: Others have done that for the very same reason.

There was another thought I had on it. Well, let me check my notes here.

I've got a list of the department heads and these may bring back some memories for you. Any of those especially?

Admiral Smith: Ford served with me in London in the CinCUSNavEur job, he was an administrative—he was OP-01; in other words, what we called it over there—B1. Wood was a Lutheran, and so we got the ship never gets to the storm with a Lutheran chaplain on board.[*]

Millett, the engineer.[†] Poor Millett shifted up to be the operations officer, and he was operations officer when the ship went aground. The captain asked him if he could leave that buoy on the starboard, and Millett said yes. Well, you could, just barely. That wasn't the way to do it, so he got hit.

Doc Murphy was with me in London again. I got a golf cart, and Murphy's a better golfer than me. He was about a 9 handicap, and I was about a 14. We went together to play at old St. Andrew's golf course. I shot 86 and he had a 92, because I

---

[*] Commander Harry C. Wood, Chaplain Corps, USN.
[†] Commander John R. Millett, USN.

listened to my caddy, and Murph thought he knew better. And we had 30 knots of wind. My face was cut with sand.

Kervin, yes, yes.[*] I was lucky I didn't have any dental problem.

McCreary—yes, a good man.[†] He came in to see me, and said, "Captain, everybody's got some silly ideas about what they like to eat and what they like in the way of dental supplies and shaving cream. So what's yours?" I thought it was a little brash, but he was a good man.

Paul Stillwell: You had Admiral Blandy on board for a while soon after you took over.[‡] What are your memories of him?

Admiral Smith: I really never knew Blandy. The first time I saw Blandy was when he was Chief of the Bureau of Ordnance, and I came back from Java.[§] He asked me to come over and tell about the experiences. And I told him about the last fight when around Bali Island.[**] He made a comment, "You know, the first gun battle since the Civil War for the U.S. Navy."

But Blandy was a splendid gunnery man. As a commander in chief, a bit aloof, I thought, but he had bad health, which nobody knew about. He had a heart problem that he worried about, I think. Anyway, he was splendid. He was a gentleman, made all the proper appearances of a flag officer. And I think he was very good. He came aboard to return my call, I guess it was. I never had him aboard for a meal, I don't think. I don't remember.

---

[*] Commander Delos R. Kervin, Dental Corps, USN.
[†] Commander Arthur D. McCreary, Supply Corps, USN.
[‡] Admiral William H. P. Blandy, USN, served as Commander in Chief Atlantic Command and Commander in Chief Atlantic Fleet from 3 February 1947 to 1 February 1950.
[§] Rear Admiral William H. P. Blandy, USN, served as Chief of the Bureau of Ordnance from February 1941 to December 1943.
[**] As a lieutenant commander, Smith was commanding officer of the destroyer *Stewart* (DD-224) at the beginning of World War II. On the night of 19-20 February 1942 she was damaged in the Battle of Bandung Strait against the Japanese.

Paul Stillwell: According to the log, he was embarked briefly for one of those fleet exercises. He had a number of his staff people come aboard, including E. P. Holmes, who was later CinCLantFlt.[*]

Admiral Smith: Yes. I can't remember that. Just skipped my mind entirely.

Unless there was something interesting happened, why, I've forgotten those routine affairs. I do remember Blandy. I remember him coming aboard the ship. I remember I was always very favorably impressed with him. And the latter part of the war, why, he'd had battleship jobs.

Paul Stillwell: He was an amphibious commander too.

Admiral Smith: Yes.

Paul Stillwell: Well, I now remember the question I was groping for before, and that was, there's been a myth that the *Missouri*'s speed was hampered by the grounding.

Admiral Smith: No.

Paul Stillwell: What was your recollection?

Admiral Smith: Well, I took command of the ship when the dry dock was being flooded. She was just about to move out. George Peckham—I went up and said, "George, I've got command."

"You what?"

I said, "Yes, I've just given my orders to the officer of the deck."

He was sort of in a state of shock. "Aye, aye, sir," he said, shook hands.

But we floated her out, and then right at the entrance to the dock we pumped oil in all night long; we got about 60,000 gallons in, I think. Then first light in the morning, we took off and went on out to sea and ran full power trials four hours—full power. And she

---

[*] Captain Ephraim P. Holmes, USN.

worked all right. We had to tie down a couple safety valves, but she made it all right. Wasn't anything wrong with her engines.

Paul Stillwell: But were there any other aftereffects in a physical sense?

Admiral Smith: No, no. Not that I'm ever aware of.

Paul Stillwell: So it was mainly the psychological damage you had to fix?

Admiral Smith: Yes, exactly. And people just lost confidence. Maybe they're going to be in trouble. That's why I decided to keep telling them, "Your only mistake is don't tell me. Don't call me." And that helped them, I know, in a little while. They came around.

Paul Stillwell: You mentioned that Admiral Wooldridge got this call when he was ComDesLant. Who was on the other end?

Admiral Smith: Admiral Fechteler. He had relieved Blandy.

Paul Stillwell: Okay, so he was CinCLantFlt.

Admiral Smith: He was CinCLantFlt. I'll never forget we were doing everything wrong. We were loading ammunition and fueling ship, which you're never supposed to do simultaneously. Again, if I'm going to get to sea at all in time to have a couple days down in Guantánamo before joining the fleet exercises—the fleet joint amphibious operations. There was a light rain, but the word came that Admiral Fechteler was going to come aboard. For God's sake, doesn't he know better than that?

So Admiral Fechteler came aboard, and no raincoat. And I was aggrieved for him, but when he stepped out of that car without a raincoat, why, I took off my raincoat. We walked up all the way around the top, and then we went down to the next level, walked from stem to stern, and when we finished twice circumnavigating the ship, why, I said, "Admiral, would you have a cup of coffee with me?"

He said, "Sure."

So we got in there, and I said, "Admiral, I want to tell you how much I appreciate what you've done. You've shown your interest in this ship to a lot of sailors that need it.

He said, "Oh, Christ," he said, "an admiral ought to be worth something." He was quite a guy, old Admiral Fechteler.

Paul Stillwell: Was he the one who made the choice that it would be you who would take command again?

Admiral Smith: Apparently, apparently. I've known Fechteler, in a funny way—can I tell you a little anecdote?

Paul Stillwell: Sure.

Admiral Smith: I'd just been back from the Far East and on Admiral King's staff for a month, I think it was, when I had orders to report to New York for special duty.[*] I got the orders on a Sunday. Real hurry up, report tomorrow morning. So I called the Bureau of Personnel, "What is this?"

"Well, you're going to be in the heroes' parade."[†]

I said, "What?"

"Yeah, they got some Britishers coming over, and we got some heroes from, you know, from guys that got medals, and you're going to tour the country to sell war bonds."

I said, "I'm not going. I'm not going. So you can start writing my general court-martial orders right now. I ain't going on any damn heroes' tour. I'm a lieutenant commander."

So Fechteler was in the Bureau of Personnel then, and he called over at Admiral King's office and got hold of one of the admirals. Said, "I got a problem. I got a guy who ain't gonna carry out orders." And I'll think of the officer's name in a minute.

---

[*] 1945 and as Commander in Chief U.S. Fleet from 20 December 1941 to 2 September 1945; he was promoted to the rank of fleet admiral in December 1944.
[†] Smith was awarded the Navy Cross for his performance in command of the *Stewart*.

Well, he said, "I'll take care of it." So he called me and told me who he was, and I was mad. He said, "Smith, now listen carefully. You will go to New York tomorrow, and you will stay 24 hours to give me time enough to get you a relief. You go 24 hours, then you can return to Washington and resume your duties. You understand that?"

I said, "Yes, sir."

So I went on up to New York and rode a ticker-tape parade. And they emptied cigarette baskets, and my God, the crap that falls out on you—it was an open car. I was riding with an English Marine who'd lost an arm. And he was crying, he was so bad. He had a bottle of whiskey in the car. He'd kneel down every now and then, take a nip out of that bottle of whiskey.

And then we went to a reception. *Time* magazine wanted to talk to me, and I told *Time* magazine what I thought about them for something they'd done. And they walked away. I was still mad. Then after the reception I was supposed to take some lovely lady, some young gal who was a debutante of the year, take her to a dance. I thought, "The hell with it." So I said, "Goodbye, I'm going home." So I caught the train and went on back home, and nobody ever said a word. So Fechteler knew who I was.

Paul Stillwell: Who told you to go for one day?

Admiral Smith: I can see him, a submariner—Edwards, Edwards, Edwards.

Paul Stillwell: Richard S. Edwards?

Admiral Smith: Yes, Dick Edwards.[*] And he looked tough. They tell the story—you know that lovely story on Edwards that King was having a little conference in his cabin, and Edwards's cabin was adjacent in Washington. And Edwards was shouting. And King said to the aide, "Who's Edwards talking to?"

The aide came back in, "He's talking to New York, sir."

"Just tell him to use the telephone."

---

[*] Rear Admiral Richard S. Edwards, USN, Deputy Chief of Staff to Commander in Chief U.S. Fleet, Admiral Ernest J. King, USN.

You've heard that story.

Paul Stillwell: I heard it attributed to someone else, Fairfax Leary.*

Admiral Smith: Well, I heard it to Edwards.

Paul Stillwell: Well, they may both have had the same problem.

Admiral Smith: Edwards was loud.

I told the story—now, I'm going to tell this last anecdote, then I'm going to quit and let you get back to your business. This one.

I don't know if I told this story about King. I was assistant to Bob Glover, who was the war planner for the Atlantic at this stage of the game.† This was early, when I first got back. They gave me other jobs later on. I was the mine warfare plans officer; I was sea frontier plans officer, all kinds of damn things. Keep you up all night sometimes.

But, at any rate, when the Japs started down the Solomons chain—it had to be in the early June, late May, whatever—they started in '42. King pronounced to us planners, "We've got to stop them. If they take the Solomons chain, they'll cut off Australia and New Zealand, and it will measurably lengthen the war. We've got to stop them. Work on it."

There was a lot of conversation, obviously, but in the last meeting with King, when he made his decision, he said again why we had to do it. And all these seniors, "Admiral, we can't do it. We haven't got it."

He said, "We've got to do it, and we're going to do it." And he said, "Kelly Turner, you're the man that knows all the reasons why we can't do it; you'll command it."‡ Now, there's the decision. I don't know whether you've seen that in the books or

---

* Rear Admiral Herbert Fairfax Leary, USN.
† Captain Robert O. Glover, USN, U.S. Fleet staff.
‡ Rear Admiral Richmond Kelly Turner, USN, was commander of the amphibious task force that invaded Guadalcanal and Tulagi in the Solomon Islands on 7 August 1942. For more details on King's decision, see Thomas B. Buell, *Master of Sea Power: A Biography of Admiral Ernest J. King* (Boston: Little, Brown, 1980).

not, because all the guys who were in that with him are dead now. And I was told by Glover when he came out and told me about it.

Paul Stillwell: Well, that was a very prescient decision on his part.

Admiral Smith: Yes. And the First Marine Division went down and fought longer and harder, and better that you'd expect a division to fight, and they held Guadalcanal.

Paul Stillwell: Especially when the United States had the Europe-first strategy.

Admiral Smith: The only time I saw King in one of these decision-making things was in the Trident conference in Washington in May of 1943. I was then in this brand-new Joint War Plans Committee. And we, Joint War Plans Committee, were allowed to come into the presence of the mighty and sit in the rear seats and listen. The British were on one side of the table, and King, Marshall on the other, with a few principal aides along with them.* Along toward the end of their meeting, why, Marshall said, "Now, gentlemen, at this meeting [this is history] we must decide precisely when we cross the channel into France. If we can't decide now, I'm not going to build up forces waiting for some indefinite period, when we can be"—better use [unclear] answer. He said, "If we can't decide at this meeting when precisely we'll go across the channel, I'll turn my attention to assist Admiral King, and we'll defeat the Japanese first."

King didn't say a word, simply nodded, looked cold across the table. The British didn't like him, you know. He didn't say a word, but it scared the hell out of them, and they decided then June 5, 1944.

Paul Stillwell: It came awfully close to that.

Admiral Smith: Well, June sixth, yes. Eisenhower put it off one day.†

---

* General of the Army George C. Marshall, USA, served as Army Chief of Staff from 1 September 1939 to 18 November 1945. He was promoted to five-star rank in December 1944.
† General of the Army Dwight D. Eisenhower, USA, was the Supreme Allied Commander in Europe in 1944-45.

Paul Stillwell: Because of the weather.

Well, you told me a story earlier about the Quebec conference in '44, when Mountbatten came over . . .

Admiral Smith: This was the Quadrant conference in August of '43.*

Paul Stillwell: Oh, I see.

Admiral Smith: And I went to sea right after that.

We had at that time, I think—except for special operations, we had in the Trident and Quadrant conferences decided the scope of the war. I really think that. I asked questions of, "How is it that King, Marshall, and Arnold won World War II with only 14 Joint Staff officers and some old staff officers—the old ones, of course—and no Secretary of Defense?"†

He said, "That's how you won it." They didn't have all that mess to fool with.

Paul Stillwell: Well, you were mentioning earlier how the decision was arrived at on the commander for the Southeast Asia theater.

Admiral Smith: Yes, it was called China-India-Burma first—CBI. It was agreed that one of the problems that Quebec was to determine was the command structure out there for future operations and for consolidating what we'd had and lost. And it was determined that the supreme commander would be a Britisher, and the deputy would be General Stilwell. Everybody knew it was going to be General Stilwell, but he would be an American.‡ The chief of staff would be an American brigadier or major general. And the three commanders—land, air, and sea—would be British.

---

* The Quadrant Conference in Quebec took place 17-24 August 1943.
† Lieutenant General Henry H. Arnold, USA, served as Commanding General of the Army Air Forces from March 1942 to March 1946. He was promoted to four-star rank in March 1943 and five-star rank in December 1944.
‡ In August 1943 Lieutenant General Joseph W. Stilwell, USA, became Deputy Supreme Allied Commander South East Asia Command under Vice Admiral Lord Louis Mountbatten, Royal Navy.

All right, that was agreed on. Then the British proposed Lord Wavell, and our people said, "No, he has an aura of defeat; he hasn't won anything. Splendid officer, of course, but he had bad luck and whatever."* Then they said Auckinleck.†

They said, "Same difference. Auckinleck is a defeated man."

So then, "You name one."

So Admiral King later named A. B. Cunningham. Cunningham knew that Dudley Pound was dying of heart disease, and he knew that he would be the next First Sea Lord, so he sent back the next dispatch saying, "This is a soldier's job."‡

So after various other names, why, Admiral King, I'm told by Admiral Savvy Cooke, King said, "Mountbatten. He's a young man full of fire and spirit, smart, and he's got the right connections."§

He said, "All right." And that's how Mountbatten got it.

Paul Stillwell: You mentioned when you brought the ship out, after she'd come out of dry dock, that you trained the crew yourself. What do you recall about the other times when you did have the fleet training people available?

Admiral Smith: I didn't have fleet training. Wait a minute, yes I did too, for a short period. On my first cruise in *Missouri*, we put into—they were good men; they were good people. And they had a strict regimen. And I think we appreciated it and liked it. But I did not have time to have them sit down and spend a day organizing their show in my ship; we had too many things to do. So for those three days, we had at Guantánamo after the grounding, why, we ran it ourselves.

Paul Stillwell: Their typical method is to come in and tell you how bad you are at the beginning . . .

---

* Field Marshal Sir Archibald Wavell, British Army.
† Lieutenant General Sir Claude Auckinleck, British Army.
‡ Admiral of the Fleet Sir Dudley Pound, Royal Navy, served as First Sea Lord from June 1939 until his death on 21 October 1943. Admiral of the Fleet Sir Andrew B. Cunningham, Royal Navy, served as First Sea Lord from October 1943 to May 1946.
§ Vice Admiral Charles M. Cooke, USN.

Admiral Smith: Oh, sure.

Paul Stillwell: . . . and how much they've improved you by the time you leave.

Admiral Smith: I didn't have time for those speeches.

Paul Stillwell: Also, on that first cruise you went down to Trinidad and the Gulf of Paria for a while. What do you remember about that trip?

Admiral Smith: Oh, I remember almost nothing except some interesting people came aboard. A Marine officer, retired, was down there on vacation of some sort, visiting some friends. And he, General Fellowes, came aboard and had—I guess I had them to a full meal. I don't remember anything about the trip down there. We had no problems, nothing.

Paul Stillwell: That's the place where the sailors have a problem drinking too much rum, then going out in the hot sun.

Admiral Smith: Yes. And get back shipboard real quick.

Paul Stillwell: There was a mention in the log about a star shell duel with USS *Rochester*.[*] Do you recall that at all?

Admiral Smith: I do remember there was one. I've forgotten. I don't remember whether we won or lost or what happened. I think it went, you know, normally.

Paul Stillwell: But you were satisfied with the gunnery operations?

---

[*] A star shell is a type of gunnery projectile that detonates in the air and provides a parachute flare for night illumination.

Admiral Smith: Oh, yes, yes. Only star shell duel I remember was with the British over in the British Far Eastern Fleet. That was a funny one.

Paul Stillwell: What's the typical way of running such a duel?

Admiral Smith: Just to see if you can illuminate the other ship and he can't escape you. I think that's all there is to it, just fairly simple.

And you have to get your star shells—if there's a cloud situation, you have to have your stars shells burst so that they either emerge from the clouds or burst under the clouds. You have to be careful about that. That's the only gunnery problem, I think.

I think the only pretty gunnery show I remember is up at Iwo Jima when they left me up there. When the last Marines left and the Army took over, an Army major came out and he said, "Sir, we know that there's Japanese in a cave down under this cliff, and we can't get to them. We know they're in there. Can you fire a bullet into the mouth of that cave?"

"Sure."

And he said, "Can you do it tomorrow?"

"Sure."

"I'll get my people out there and mow them down when they come out if you chase them out."

So I took my flag boat *Dunlap* in to do this; I wanted to see it myself. And he got himself all lined up and had his riflemen aim at the mouth. They could see down this cliff that I think was about 100 feet. Quite a high one. They couldn't possibly have got down there. And even if they'd gone in by boats, assault landing, they still would have been shot up pretty badly by the Japs. So *Dunlap* fired one into the mouth of the cave, and nothing happened. So I told them, "Try a star shell."

So they just said, "Was that round loaded?"

"Yeah, it was loaded and went in. Saw the tracer."

He said, "Fire two." So the *Dunlap* fired a star shell in with the phosphorus. And here come the Japs, and the Army shot 120 of them.

Paul Stillwell: Gee.

Admiral Smith: That's the kind of shooting you like to look at.

Paul Stillwell: Sure.

I guess a star shell duel, though, is sort of an anachronism in the age of radar.

Admiral Smith: Yes, it's no good at all. You have to put a gun so that [unclear]. It's a little exercise in fire control. Pretty show, nothing really useful about it.

Paul Stillwell: Any recollections of the visit to Panama?

Admiral Smith: Panama cruise, I remember just drill, drill, drill, and the weather was perfect.[*] We went into Panama, and I had four guests of the Secretary of the Navy aboard—there's a picture of them in there; I don't remember these gentlemen except they were all businessmen, all important ones. Very nice people. And they used to play gin rummy in my cabin while I was on the bridge all the time. Nice people.

Then in Panama, no troubles, no problems, no shoot-outs. Oh, I do remember one thing. In Panama they have a two-number lottery—two digits. So I was ashore just to see the place on the east coast. I bought a number 63, and it came in and won $40.00, so I bought a Panama hat.[†] My only experience in Panama.

Paul Stillwell: Did you get visitors in places like that also?

Admiral Smith: Some, not many, not much, no. They're too used to seeing those big boats go through there. Not much interest.

Paul Stillwell: The *Missouri* by that point was the only battleship left in commission. Was there pressure to decommission her as well?

---

[*] The *Missouri* visited Cristobal, Panama Canal Zone, from 30 April to 2 May 1949.
[†] The hull number of the *Missouri* was BB-63.

Admiral Smith: I don't think so, not with Mr. Truman as President, no, no. I walked out of the White House when I went over for some reason. I went over to see Admiral Leahy, I guess.[*] He had a picture of *Missouri*, so I took that one away with me with his permission.

I buried Admiral Leahy. I was in charge of his funeral. I was in charge of Halsey's funeral, too, as Chief of Personnel.[†]

Paul Stillwell: They both died in 1959.[‡]

Admiral Smith: Yes. When we buried Halsey, it was the prettiest thing you've ever seen in the Episcopal cathedral there.[§] All the great old men of our time were gathered—Admiral Hart, and so on.[**] President Eisenhower had to be away from the city on something, so he asked Admiral Nimitz to represent him.[††] With the cathedral all in place, the honorary pallbearers—all old men—in place, in came Nimitz in white uniform and walked to the bier and bowed over it for about a minute, and there wasn't a dry eye in the house, it was so pretty. I was sitting by Mrs. Halsey; she'd asked me to.

Then when it was over, I got back to my office and trying to catch up with some work, and there was a great hullabaloo in the outer office—Admiral Nimitz. In he came, and I said, "Admiral Nimitz, can I get you anything?"

"No, you can't get me anything; I've just got a little time with my daughter, and I've got to go back west." "But," he said, "there's something you can do for me. Two things. First, I know that General Marshall is going to die soon; he's dying. I know the Army's going to ask me to come back, and I just must not. I can't do another one. The next funeral of a five-star officer I attend is going is going to be in San Francisco."[‡‡] He meant himself. I made all the proper exclamations.

---

[*] Admiral William D. Leahy, USN, served as chief of staff to the President (in his capacity as Commander in Chief of the Armed Forces) from July 1942 to March 1949. Leahy was promoted to the five-star rank of fleet admiral in December 1944.
[†] As a vice Admiral Smith served as Chief of Naval Personnel from 31 January 1958 to 12 February 1960.
[‡] Leahy died on 20 July 1959 and Halsey died 16 August 1959.
[§] Fleet Admiral William F. Halsey Jr., USN (Ret.).
[**] Admiral Thomas C. Hart, USN (Ret.).
[††] Fleet Admiral Chester W. Nimitz, USN.
[‡‡] General of the Army George C. Marshall, USA, died 16 October 1959.

He said, "No, no. Now, number two, I want you to go to Chairman Vinson, Carl Vinson, and remind him that when we created the five-star officers, there was debate about whether the last one would go to Halsey or Spruance. Admiral Halsey, of course, got the five stars, well deserved. But Admiral Spruance, also, was a splendid officer. Now, they're all dead except me [of the five-star officers]. Spruance is an old man; it won't cost the country very much to promote him now to five stars. Ask the chairman if he won't promote him now."*

So immediately—as soon as Nimitz left, I called the chairman and said that, "Admiral Nimitz had sent his deepest respects and abject apologies, he can't come and pay his respects to the chairman. But would he—" and then I went on with the story.

He said, "Come down at 7:00 o'clock in the morning." That's when he threw out anybody he didn't want to see.

"Yes, sir, I'll be there." So I went to see him at 7:00.

And you know, he wore those half-glasses, put them on his nose and said, "Now, tell me, who are the five-star admirals?" So I told him. "And who were the five-star generals?" So I told him. He knew; he was just thinking what he was going to tell me. "And now, they were all created during World War II."

I said, "No, sir," I said, "General Bradley was created after 1947."

"Oh, yeah," he said, "That's Chairman of the Joint Chiefs. We did that. That was a mistake; we shouldn't have done that. We should leave that exalted rank for a major war." So he said, "You tell Admiral Nimitz with my deepest respect and my best hopes, and so on, that we're going to leave it just like it is."

Paul Stillwell: And so it remained.

Admiral Smith: Yes.

---

* Representative Carl Vinson (Democrat-Georgia) was Chairman of the House Armed Services Committee. Admiral Raymond A. Spruance, USN (Ret.), lived until 1969. He was not promoted to five-star rank. See Thomas B. Buell, *The Quiet Warrior: A Biography of Admiral Raymond A. Spruance* (Boston: Little, Brown, 1974), pages 435-436

Paul Stillwell: So it was apparent to you, then, that it had been a real emotional burden for Admiral Nimitz to go to that funeral?

Admiral Smith: It was. It was emotional to us just looking at him. It really was.

Paul Stillwell: Well, that says something about his loyalty to Halsey.

Admiral Smith: Yes.

In the old book, the battleships—I had it around here once—it tells of Halsey's Third Fleet sinking the *Musashi* when Kurita was a Jap admiral in the Sibuyan Sea.[*] I was with Admiral John Sidney McCain in the fast carrier task force.[†] I was in a destroyer squadron. We had been away from port for about three months. And we were down to beans and rice, really. There wasn't anything left in our frozen lockers. So we were detached to head back to Ulithi. I was reading the dispatches, and Halsey had decided that Kurita's force was defeated and turned back. And he'd gone up to the north to chase down Ozawa.[‡]

We went to general quarters always at sunset, just to be sure. That was the dangerous time when a submarine might get to you. So we secured for general quarters, and a whole mess of young officers were on the bridge. I remember sounding off to my officers. I said, "You're going to see tonight the last chance missed of battleships sinking battleships, because Kurita's coming out; he's coming out sure as hell. And Halsey's not going to be there. Willis Lee with his battleships will miss it.[§]

And sure enough—but we were well on our way. Hell, we were a day away from there, I guess, or almost a day—from Leyte, when we were ordered back to Leyte, best

---

[*] On 24 October 1944, during the Battle of Leyte Gulf, carrier aircraft from the Third Fleet sank the Japanese super battleship *Musashi* in the Sibuyan Sea in the Philippines. Admiral Halsey was then Commander Third Fleet. Vice Admiral Takeo Kurita was in command of the Japanese surface force.

[†] Vice Admiral John S. McCain, USN, Commander Task Group 38.1

[‡] On 24-25 October 1944, as part of the wide-ranging Battle of Leyte Gulf, he steamed north with Task Force 38, the fleet's carrier striking force and supporting ships. His objective was to sink a force of Japanese aircraft carriers under Vice Admiral Jisaburo Ozawa. He unwittingly left San Bernardino Strait unguarded for a foray by Japanese battleships and cruisers. The Japanese surface ships eventually turned around and went back after encountering a plucky U.S. force of escort carriers and destroyers.

[§] Vice Admiral Willis A. Lee Jr., USN, was to have been in command of a surface task force, but it wasn't formed until it was too late.

speed, because we were closer than Halsey was at that time. And we got back in time just simply to launch a strike, which turned to Kurita. He didn't know what was there with him; he didn't know whether it was Halsey or what. But, at any rate, I do remember that the captains in the carriers were saying, "Admiral, we can't quite make it." He wanted to launch much too quick. But they didn't do much damage to Kurita, because these guys were on the prowl to get the hell back. And, even so, my destroyers picked up something like 15 aviators. But it did turn Kurita, went on back.

Paul Stillwell: I read a commentary that Admiral Kinkaid wrote.[*] He said, "I can imagine the frustration that my classmate Lee felt steaming 300 miles north and 300 south and not firing a shot."

Admiral Smith: Yes. It was a shame.

I do remember my advice to the young officers, "Remember this night; we're going to miss that one opportunity."

Paul Stillwell: That's exactly the way it happened.

Admiral Smith: Of course, at Surigao Strait, we did sink a couple battleships.[†]

Paul Stillwell: You were talking about your GQ at dusk for submarines, the fleet exercise in the spring of 1950 was an ASW type exercise—Portrex, I think it was called. Do you have any recollections of that specifically? What does a battleship captain do, just rely on the screen?

Admiral Smith: Sure, sure. Oh, yes, I do remember that—no, no, then was when I was PhibGroup 2.[‡] I had one of those operations. And, of course, the old amphibious ships, the AKs and APs were so slow, you couldn't do much whatever to—I think there was an

---

[*] Vice Admiral Thomas C. Kinkaid, USN, was Commander Seventh Fleet during the battle. He was a Naval Academy classmate of Vice Admiral Lee.
[†] The Battle of Surigao Strait, which took place the night of 24-25 October 1944, was the last naval surface engagement that pitted battleships of opposing navies against each other.
[‡] Amphibious Group Two.

atomic bomb scare there. You had to scatter and then come back together again, which was always a mess.

Paul Stillwell: Did you have any doctrine for radiological defense in the *Missouri*?

Admiral Smith: No, not really. Didn't pay much attention to it.

As I recall, we just simply weren't equipped to defend against it. So if you got hit with it, you've had it.

Paul Stillwell: Was there any wash-down system for getting rid of fallout?

Admiral Smith: Yes, you had that kind of thing for the cleanup. But we simply didn't have the equipment or didn't have the clothing or any of that for the crew.

I've got a very poor memory, I think, about things that just went routine.

Paul Stillwell: What do you remember about Norfolk as a homeport for the ship?

Admiral Smith: Well, for me it was very good, because I think my wife and I were the first couple to come down of any of the captains. They never had a couple come down. The wives stayed up in Washington, wherever they lived. And the captains came down, spent weekends going back up to Washington. My wife came down, and I instituted the calls and return calls.[*] They all called, and Dee and I would return there them. Some of them were pretty funny. We got them broken into what I regard as the old customs and manners.

Paul Stillwell: In what ways were they funny?

Admiral Smith: Oh, you might go to a lieutenant commander's house at 5:00 o'clock of a Sunday afternoon, and he'd open the door in his undershirt. He wanted to close the

---

[*] In the pre-World War II period, it was customary for a ship's officers to pay a visit on the commanding officer and his wife, and then the captain and his wife would pay a return visit.

door on you. "Leave the door open. Let me have a drink, and go and put a shirt on." Laugh at him.

But I don't know whether they liked it or not, but they went through it.

Paul Stillwell: Well, it was certainly a custom that you had grown up with.

Admiral Smith: Oh, yes.

Paul Stillwell: What level of rank did you go down to in those calls?

Admiral Smith: Oh, everyone that was married. The unmarried officers were supposed to come call on me and say goodbye. I didn't call on them.

I haven't answered your question about the homeport. In the course of this, we had receptions for civilians in Norfolk. We knew some; we knew several girls who married in the Navy. As a matter of fact, my best friend, Bob Sutcliffe, married a girl from Norfolk. And his daughter is my Godchild. So we knew families already down there.

Paul Stillwell: Well, there's that famous old saying about Norfolk, "Sailors and dogs keep away." How did your crew feel about the city?

Admiral Smith: Oh, I think they liked it all right. If they didn't have Norfolk, they'd go on up to Richmond. But I think that Norfolk had plenty of amenities for the sailor.

Paul Stillwell: Well, that famous area of Granby and East Main was pretty bad.

Admiral Smith: Pretty bad—red light.

Paul Stillwell: And bars up and down both sides of the streets.

Admiral Smith: Well, the sailor didn't have very much money in those days. You know, the seaman second class got $36.00 a month.

I was looking at something or other—orders—when I went over to Eisenhower's staff in June of 1943, and I was given $6.00 a day for food—$6.00 a day.

Paul Stillwell: How times have changed.

Admiral Smith: Yes, I don't know what they get today. It's quite a lot then.

Paul Stillwell: On the discipline, that's one of the roles of the captain, of course, to hold mast, and I found numerous instances in the log. It seemed to me that the thing that you awarded most often was extra duty and restrictions and occasionally the brig. How would you characterize discipline in general in the ship?

Admiral Smith: I think it was quite good. We had good petty officers. It was the only battleship. We tried to instill that idea into them, "This is the President's own personal battleship, and try to keep it as clean as you can." Have the men dress as well as they could. I was used to that, and I'll diverge again. When I took command of the *Stewart* in Manila in May of 1940, she stood 13 in 13 ships, and she was dirty.* And I went to work right away on that one. The previous captain was a hell of a nice guy—he's dead now, Deke Evans—but he just let things go adrift.†

Anyway, I cleaned her up and made so much noise, apparently, the word got around so much that when it came my annual inspection, which was normally held by the squadron commander, Admiral Hart came and inspected my ship.‡ And I remember the first comment I had to him was when we went into the officers' galley. He had said in his nasal twang, "Any cockroaches in this galley, steward?"

I spoke up and said, "No, sir. No cockroaches in this galley."

---

* USS *Stewart* (DD-224), a *Clemson*-class destroyer, was commissioned 15 September 1920. Displacement was 1,215 tons, length 314 feet, and beam of 32 feet. Top speed was 35 knots. She was armed with four 4-inch guns, one 3-inch gun, and 12 21-inch torpedo tubes.
† Lieutenant Commander Donald S. Evans, USN, commanded the ship in 1939-40.
‡ Admiral Thomas C. Hart, USN, served as Commander in Chief U.S. Asiatic Fleet from 25 July 1939 to 4 February 1942.

He said, "There's cockroaches in every galley."

I said, "Admiral, cockroaches are afraid to live in this ship." That word got around. But I did clean the ship up. And I started with the galley, with the crew's galley. And the crew watched that. And I worked on uniforms.

Then war came along, I remember I made our crew go into clean white uniforms at mess time in the evening. And they groused about it. First the other ships threw away the whites and all wore dungarees, though. I remember we got down to Surabaya, and I heard the sailors say to men from another ship, "You've got to go over to that crap house next door." They said, "It's just dirty." And they were proud of it. So when you get them started with the idea of being proud of being good, why, they like it.

Paul Stillwell: Well, that was a special motivational tool you had in the *Missouri*, the only battleship.

Admiral Smith: The only battleship. Oh, little things. I ordered some expensive stationery with the battleship *Missouri* name and the commission pennant—rather expensive stationery for those days, maybe $2.50 or $3.00. And you know who bought it? Sailors.

Paul Stillwell: It made them feel special.

Admiral Smith: Sure. Sailors bought it.

Paul Stillwell: There was on the second of September 1949 a ceremony honoring the fourth anniversary of the surrender. What are your recollections of that?

Admiral Smith: I do remember that Admiral Smith wanted to have it very special. He wanted plenty of pictures; he wanted to send them to General MacArthur, which we did.* He and his staff arranged that amphitheater all around the surrender plaque.

Paul Stillwell: That's a very impressive photo.

Admiral Smith: Yes, it's very pretty. But he did that personally. And I guess I was on the bridge. I don't think I was in the thing. But he was very pleased with that and sent it off to MacArthur. I think MacArthur answered.

Paul Stillwell: Well, you said that he sent three sets of photos to the ship from the surrender.

Admiral Smith: Yes. I asked him for that.

Paul Stillwell: Do you have any recollections of Admiral Smith's staff members and your dealings with them?

Admiral Smith: Oh, well, Roland Smoot was the chief of staff once, and Goat Mendenhall—they're both dead now—was the other one.† Two of them in my time, both of friends, both of them a class ahead of me. I knew them very well. And so no problem there at all, never.

    I think Goat told me on occasion my ship looked dirty, and I had to agree with him. "We're working on it."

Paul Stillwell: That, apparently, was before you got your program into effect.

---

*. On 14 August 1945 President Truman announced the designation of General of the Army Douglas MacArthur as Supreme Commander of the Allied Powers for the occupation and surrender of Japan. He presided over the 2 September 1945 surrender ceremony on board the *Missouri*.
† Captain Roland T. Smoot, USN; Captain William K. Mendenhall Jr., USN. The oral history of Smoot, who retired as a vice admiral, is in the Naval Institute collection.

Admiral Smith: Well, it never was, really, what I wanted to see, and you never could make the ship with the World War II paint look like those pretty things before World War II. It was the old war color.

Paul Stillwell: Did you holystone the decks?[*]

Admiral Smith: Oh, yes. You didn't use a holystones as much as you used to in the old battleships, simply because we didn't want to wear the deck out. But you did use sand and soap. So the decks were kept fairly white. They were pretty good. But I was never happy about the paint, never.

Paul Stillwell: What do you recall about personnel inspections?

Admiral Smith: We divided the ship into sections, and I'd have the executive and the heads of departments inspect various sections of the ship. And we'd, of course, run a routine so that the ship's orderly, and then always got their inspection. And quickly. If you did it that way, you'd have everybody inspected it simultaneously, you know, why, it was over, and they could go on and go ashore.

Paul Stillwell: It's deadly if they have to wait for the captain to inspect 1,600 guys.

Admiral Smith: It's long.

Paul Stillwell: Did they meet your standards on appearance?

Admiral Smith: I think so, yes. Yes, I remember being happy about them—and a perfectly splendid Marine detachment, I remember.

And one nice story about the Marines. On that three-day trip to Guantánamo one morning—the morning maybe we were leaving, why, two Marines were on report, and

---

[*] Holystoning refers to the practice of cleaning a ship's wooden decks by scraping them with bricks pushed back and forth across the planks by means of wooden handles. It is a laborious operation.

they were two of my orderlies. On report for fighting in the bus coming back from the crew's recreation center to the dock. And, funny thing, the top sergeant never appeared at mast with any other Marines, but he was up there on this one. So I knew that this was really special in the top sergeant's heart. So I held the Marines until the last, when everybody else had gone, and I said, "What happened?"

"Oh, sir," he said, "we were just riding. I heard somebody say 'that Mudbank Mo,' and I says to my friend, I says, 'We're going to have trouble.'"

I said, "Right there's where you should have got off the bus."

"Oh, but, sir, and so I was—" And he went on talking.

I told him again, "Well, you should have gotten off that bus and not waited for that fight to happen. Sure you could fight. I'm not saying a Marine can't fight. But you didn't have to fight those sailors. They were just drunk and wanted to start something."

"When they called it mud—"

"Yeah, I know, Mudbank Mo. You're both going to get ten hours' extra duty." And the top sergeant turned then and went away. I knew I did exactly right.

Paul Stillwell: Was that a problem for a while afterward, that people were poking fun at the ship for running aground?

Admiral Smith: Not long, no. I don't recall ever having much of a problem; I tried to stop that. It was probably grandstanding. I really did act like a jackass on occasion, burned a lot more fuel than you needed to, and so and so. But it had an effect; it was exactly what I wanted—a first-class ship again.

Paul Stillwell: How did you perceive that you were being successful?

Admiral Smith: Simply because the criticism and the laughing died down; it just quit. She was a warship again.

Paul Stillwell: You probably had something of a difficulty keeping a straight face when those Marines were telling their story.

Admiral Smith: Oh, yes, yes. Had to look real serious.

Paul Stillwell: Do you have any other amusing cases in the *Missouri*?

Admiral Smith: I don't think so, no.

Paul Stillwell: I found one situation in the log, where the sailor was made a prisoner at large or something because he was suspected of being a bigamist.

Admiral Smith: Can't remember that one. In my time?

Paul Stillwell: Yes, sir.

Admiral Smith: I can't remember that. I know I've had to make a sailor go ashore and marry a girl but I . . .

Paul Stillwell: How does the captain make him marry somebody?

Admiral Smith: Oh, just simple. You say, "Got this report that you've got a little girl, So-and-so, and she's pregnant. And she says you did it."
    "Oh, no, sir."
    "Well," I said, "how long you been going with her?"
    "Well,"—named a time.
    I said, "Do you sleep with this girl?"
    "Sure."
    "Well," I said, "what do you think those things are for, for god's sake? Was anybody else going with her?"
    "No, nobody else was going with her."
    "Why don't you go up there and marry the girl then? She's yours."
    "All right."

Paul Stillwell: The *Missouri*, of course, got some bad press after she went aground. How much dealing did you have with news people?

Admiral Smith: None. I'm not very good with press. I give them facts if it's appropriate. I do remember that as we steamed out of Portsmouth shipyard, there were several yachts following me with cameras grinding to see the *Missouri* run aground again. And the newspaper said the next morning that *Missouri*'s back to normal, something like that—that she exited and entered again without any problem.

Paul Stillwell: Were you in any way involved in the court of inquiry for the other officers?

Admiral Smith: They never asked me; they never asked me. They did need expert testimony: what the ship could do; could she have gone, you know, left or right of that buoy—the Army's ground mine defense system battery. They needed someone to give them expert information on how the ship was handled, what she could do, and instead of asking me they asked the yard pilot. It's all right. And, you know, the yard pilot, they took the youngest one, the junior member. I asked him about it later and he said, "Oh, hell, somebody had to do it so I'm Joe, I'm the young one.

Paul Stillwell: Well, he probably didn't want to do it any more than you did.

Admiral Smith: No, no. But they never asked me to—never went down there.
    Of course, the classmate situation was probably—I don't know.[*]

Paul Stillwell: Well, he felt bad about it, and you would have felt bad being involved in it.
    You mentioned harbor pilots. In general, how much did you use them?

---

[*] Captain Brown and Captain Smith were in the Naval Academy class of 1924.

Admiral Smith: Normally used them just to put the ship in alongside the dock. We had to use several tugs, of course, to pull her out and get her straightened away. Then the pilot would say, "Have a good cruise, Captain," and off we'd go.

Paul Stillwell: Did they know the ship as well as you did?

Admiral Smith: They had the tugs in, and yes, they knew it well enough. They were good men. And she wasn't difficult. As I keep saying, she was easy enough, you just remember that she got all that power—212,000 horsepower—and the double rudders and four screws, she could move in any direction, except backing.

Paul Stillwell: Did you have any problems other than the one you mentioned in shallow water, where you couldn't twist her in Guantánamo?

Admiral Smith: You could get the same sort of run-out in Hampton Roads. If you tried to turn—I remember once having to leave port and fog set in. So I anchored in Hampton Roads before entering Thimble Shoals Channel. She'd swung to the tide, and I had considerable trouble, stirred up a lot of mud twisting her, getting her headed around again. So she didn't do well in shallow water.

Paul Stillwell: You took her to Annapolis a couple times. Any special recollections of those visits?

Admiral Smith: I took her to Annapolis only once. Yes. I took her up in June—early June of 1949 for the first midshipman cruise, and I had to get her down to 30-feet draft, because York Spit Channel was 32 foot. And I do remember that that's when I learned the hard way that you've got to keep a lot of weight forward. So I left all the fuel that we left on board—I left that forward, and actually put water in the peak tanks to keep her bow down. That got her down to 30 feet. But then that was a long, laborious process. So after that cruise was back, why, the midshipmen were brought down to Norfolk for the second cruise. I only went up there once.

Paul Stillwell: What did you do, off-load your fuel into barges?

Admiral Smith: No, no, just pumped it out alongside the dock.

Paul Stillwell: I see.

Admiral Smith: Pumped it back into the tanks.

Paul Stillwell: Why did you want her to be drawing more forward?

Admiral Smith: Well, because she's down by the stern 17 feet, when she's empty of all liquids. That's what they didn't remember when they started to lighten her. They should have left quite a lot of weight forward, so that the stern would come up the same as the bow. But they off-loaded all the liquids and all ammunition.

Paul Stillwell: Were there any special considerations putting her into and out of dry dock?

Admiral Smith: Not that I know of. She did have a rip in her—not a bad one—but she had a rip in her bottom, right across some old piece of steel down there. And that was repaired. But she had no damage to rudders or to screws, I recall. I wasn't there, of course; they were already finished that when I took command.

Paul Stillwell: I was thinking of just the process of getting her in and out. She was in dry dock in the fall of '49, before the collision. Is that a case where you had a special docking pilot?

Admiral Smith: Yes. Now I was permitted to take the ship over to Portsmouth from Norfolk after the pilot took me away from the dock and turned me around.* I could go over without a pilot and without tugs.

---

* The Norfolk Naval Shipyard is in Portsmouth, Virginia.

But not to be recommended, because I remember one time going over, just as I got where I was going to make the turn around the coal docks, out backed a steamer. Well, you can't move *Missouri* sideways. We had a little problem there for several minutes. But you should not do that; you should take tugs with you. I would recommend that to anyone.

Paul Stillwell: And then for the last stage, the docking pilot gets her in on the keel blocks.

Admiral Smith: By Navy law you must turn over the ship to the docking pilot and to the docking officer. And he takes her in, oh, from the end of—I can't describe it, but where the Navy yard property begins is where the yard pilot takes the control.

Paul Stillwell: I see.

Admiral Smith: Now, you can take it away from him if he's running into trouble. A skipper can always take her away from him, because you always have that amount of responsibility.

I took a ship away from a pilot in New York Harbor coming out. He was a new pilot, and he was so happy; he'd never been aboard the *Missouri*. He was telling all about how good he was or something, and something went wrong—I've forgotten now what it was—but I had to take the ship from him. As soon as I straightened it out—whatever it was, too close to another ship, I think—I gave it back to him and apologized for it. But he straightened out then and kept his eyes on the ball.

Paul Stillwell: How responsive was the engineering plant? Did you have to give any warnings to build up steam?

Admiral Smith: No. None, nothing.

Paul Stillwell: Well, you talked about burning more fuel than usual. Was there, in general, a restriction on speed?

Admiral Smith: Oh, yes, economy, you know. As a matter of fact, part of your battle efficiency pennant was your economy in fuel consumption. So I didn't pay much attention to fuel, just for those grandstand times. I don't know why I keep referring to that, but it was important. I had to make the ship feel that they could be proud of it again and let folks know that this ain't any slowpoke.

Paul Stillwell: You talked about underway replenishment and going up and down half a turn occasionally. Are there any other special considerations involved? Did you ever replenish your ammunition?

Admiral Smith: No, no, only fuel oil. Never anything else. You could, I guess, but it'd be pretty slow and laborious to take 2,700-pound shells.

Paul Stillwell: Do you have any recollections of the loading or unloading process in port, then, for the ammunition?

Admiral Smith: Yes, as I say, when we were loading her up again after the full-power trials, after the grounding, why, we had everything going on at once—everything, which is not proper. But we had double watches out everywhere to be sure, because we had to get it done.

Paul Stillwell: You have to be very concerned about safety so that fingers don't get mashed and that kind of thing.

Admiral Smith: Yes. But everybody was anxious to do that. It was a big job. They'd been sitting there and sitting there, watching their misery quite a number of days out there in the mud bank.

Paul Stillwell: Well, it's really touching to see the log entries: "Aground as before."

Admiral Smith: Yes, yes.

Paul Stillwell: What do you recall about the captain's mess and some of the guests you had?

Admiral Smith: Oh, I've got only one picture in there of a Spanish lady—Victoria Nanosan Hedes. She's still a respected soprano. She came aboard and we paid her; I mean, there's a fee. We paid her to come aboard in Portsmouth and sing to the crew. I had been off to some party; I couldn't attend her concert. But as soon as it was over, I was back aboard, whatever it was. The British had me somewhere. I asked her up into my cabin with her husband, who was her manager, and a very charming person.

Paul Stillwell: Did you have very capable stewards?

Admiral Smith: Yes, excellent. I remember my first two or three days aboard *Missouri*, I was getting an awful lot of potatoes and beans and things. So I told somebody, "I don't want so much starch now; I'm going to get too fat and heavy. So cut down on the starch." So the next meal I had spaghetti. [Laughter] They didn't know much about diets.

Paul Stillwell: I guess they learned.

Admiral Smith: Gullito—I'll never forget, Gullito.

Paul Stillwell: What do you remember about the quality of your chief petty officers and other enlisted men. Did *Missouri* get special call on talent?

Admiral Smith: I don't think they got special call. No, not special. Run-of-the mill isn't right. They were good people. But I don't believe that anybody had really . . .

Paul Stillwell: Not handpicked.

Admiral Smith: Not handpicked, no. I never picked anybody. I never have in all my life picked—except just once, just once in my life I picked a person. That was my pilot in England. If I didn't bring him back here and keep him with me, why, he would be released from the Navy without retirement. If I could keep him here, Atlantic Fleet, I could get him to 18 years, and then they'd keep him. That's the only person I've ever asked for, and he came back from England with me.

Paul Stillwell: You mentioned the one shore bombardment where you hit the waterline at Vieques. Do you have any other memories of shore bombardments?

Admiral Smith: Not shore bombardment, no. She had a beautiful fire control system and very accurate. All she needed to know was the information, and then once she fired and a spot was made, then she could hit the next one.

The story goes—I don't know where I've seen it—I remember that President Truman was told the *Missouri* had fired seven rounds at some target in Korea, I believe, and had six hits. And he answered his aide with a straight face, said, "What happened to the other round?"

Aide said, "Oh, sir, a ranging shot."

"Well," he said, "You tell them those things are expensive; tell them to be careful with them." [Laughter] That was his sense of humor.

Paul Stillwell: How much contact, if any, did you have with the state of Missouri itself?

Admiral Smith: People would come from Missouri, and I would try to do something with them, and they made me—oh, hell, they'd give me a hog-calling member of their band or whatever. I got a lot of those things, which I'll never forget, because the only keepsake I've got is that Missouri book.

Paul Stillwell: Did you ever go out to visit the state?

Admiral Smith: Not during my time of command. I went to visit the state when I was the Deputy Chief of Information. I was that for one year, and I did a lot of traveling then. That was the year of my life I said I was playing a piano in the red-light district. I was up there working for Wooldridge, and Wooldridge got pulled out to go down to the Joint Staff, because he'd been OP-35, as I told you. Spike Fahrion came up to be ComDesLant, and I was just getting along fine with Spike.* He hadn't asked for me to be chief of staff. He looked me over for a few days; I've never known him. And I knew he couldn't make the first move, so I just said, "Admiral, I know that you need a chief of staff. If you ever pick somebody, I apply for the job."

He said, "You got it." Just like that. Well, we were getting along fine. Spike Fahrion was a splendid officer and a tough one too. But all of a sudden, I got ordered down to Washington to be interviewed by the SecNav, Matthews.† This would have been late '50. I just got back in running the destroyer business pretty well, I thought, getting ships on off to—we had to send a couple destroyers over to Korea, go over to the Pacific Fleet. I got down to Matthews, and he said, "Have you ever been an aide?"

"No, sir."

"Have you ever been in information?"

"No, sir."

"Would you like that job?

"No, sir."

He said, "You got it. You're just the guy I want."

Then I found out that Rear Admiral Bob Hickey, who was Chief of Information, had gone over to BuPers to find out who probably would be selected on the next selection board.‡ He said, "I've got to get out of here, too, you know, so you're it."

Well, I got selected and I went to Wu Duncan, Vice Chief, and said, "I want a job; I want to go to sea."§

---

* Rear Admiral Frank G. Fahrion, USN, commanded Destroyer Force Atlantic Fleet from 27 July 1950 to 2 January 1952.
† Francis P. Matthews served as Secretary of the Navy from 25 May 1949 to 30 July 1951.
‡ Rear Admiral Robert F. Hickey, USN, served as the Navy's Chief of Information from September 1950 to July 1952.
§ Admiral Donald B. Duncan, USN, served as Vice Chief of Naval Operations from 10 August 1951 to 1 September 1956. His oral history is in the Columbia University collection.

He was already figuring on where he was going to send us new selectees. He said, "Page, I didn't intend to send you to sea, yet, anyway. I got something else in mind. I'll tell you about it."

"Thank you, sir."

"Yes, sir."

I went out, and he sent me down to the office of Secretary of Defense as a rear admiral. I put on the uniform, you know, spot promotion—and captain's pay, of course—to be the Director of the Office of Foreign Military Affairs. And at that time there was one other flag officer, Navy, in the office of the Secretary of Defense, and he was a lawyer. About five years ago, I looked at the organization of the Pentagon, and there were 17 flag officers in the office of the Secretary of Defense, and a vice admiral was deputy to the guy who had my job when I was rear admiral. He was a civilian right out of Harvard, I guess. These were overloaded down there. Just silly.

At any rate, I worked down there for Frank Nash, a wonderful man who died very early.* He would have been Secretary of State instead of Dean Rusk if he lived.† He was that much better than Rusk. Rusk won't sue, either, because he knows what I think of him.

Paul Stillwell: Well, anything else to add about the *Missouri*. I think I've about exhausted my list of questions. Any other experiences that stand out in your mind—amusing or otherwise?

Admiral Smith: No, but tonight I'll probably think of several anecdotes that I might well have told you.

Paul Stillwell: Oh, I was wondering about the role of athletics in the ship. That was certainly a big thing between the world wars with smokers and football and baseball. How much of that was still around when you had command?

---

* Frank C. Nash served as Assistant Secretary of Defense (International Security Affairs) from 11 February 1953 to 28 February 1954.
† Dean Rusk served as Secretary of State from 21 January 1961 to 20 January 1969.

Admiral Smith: We did not have a football team. And a young Catholic chaplain—I asked for an assistant chaplain and a Catholic—by golly, I can see the man—wonderful man. I'm afraid it's gone. But he wanted to raise a football team; he'd been a football player himself. And he wanted to raise it when we went to the shipyard in the fall of '49. I wouldn't permit it. We did have baseball and basketball and like that—inexpensive sports that don't require a great, huge amount of training or equipment. Any guy can play baseball, he thinks, you know, sandlot—and basketball. And there was a lot of interest. I don't think it was quite as well organized then as it is now.

Paul Stillwell: Well, it was certainly not as important as it was in the fleet of the '30s, let's say.

Admiral Smith: Oh, no. All those whaleboat races, everything, everything. When I went over to the Base Force, I had to become the coach of a football team, and I was not a football player. I entered the Naval Academy at the age of 16; I weighed 120-odd pounds. When I graduated, I weighed 150-odd, and I grew three inches in the Naval Academy. So I wasn't a football player. I wasn't much of anything. I went out for all the class sports. I was always out for something, trying. But to be a football coach for a team in San Pedro, California—no. Somebody was just a bit silly. But the sailors liked it; they joined it.

Paul Stillwell: What role did the chaplains in the *Missouri* play for you?

Admiral Smith: Of course, the Catholic had confessions. He did very well at it. But the chaplains did work hard. I did not put the chaplains in charge of beer parties. I let some redneck officer take that one, not the chaplain.

A lot of ships, you know, that was the chaplain's job. He was the morale officer. I never put the chaplain in charge of a beer party, because you can get some funny ones on a beer party—somebody needs to be knocked out, you know.

Paul Stillwell: Did you have smokers on the fantail with boxing and so forth?

Admiral Smith: Yes, very much, very much. On each one of the midshipman cruises, we had contests of very sorts—acey-deucey, bridge, checkers, anything, as well as boxing—the smoker, the real smoker.* But we didn't have wrestling. That was a little beyond us. But a lot of boxing. And after those bouts were over, then we'd give out prizes to the acey-deucey players.

I'll never forget on the *Missouri* when I gave out the prize to the chief petty officer who'd won the acey-deucey championship, I had to say something funny. It was coming back from Cuba, and the sea was clear and so on. I said, "Chief, you're not champion of the *Missouri* till you've played me."

He stuck his nose in the mike and said, "Captain, I'll play you any day, any time." They cheered—the crew all thought that was funny.

Actually, the crew, the crew asked me down for lunch one day, and in about ten minutes they finished their lunch. I thought, "Lord, I can't get up and leave now." So I talked to them, I said, "You know, there's a chief in here calls himself a champion. I want to play him acey-deucey." And, "Yea!"—they're all for it. And the chief was really good, but luck would have it, I got a string of acey-deuceys right when I was about to be beaten, and I beat him. And the chiefs all thought that was fun.

Paul Stillwell: How good a group of chiefs did you have?

Admiral Smith: Splendid, splendid. And I think the chiefs had been downplayed a bit and just not enough attention paid to them. I paid a lot of attention to the chiefs, and they liked that. I have a little silver plate out there that the chief petty officers of the *Missouri* gave me.

Paul Stillwell: How did you go about manifesting that attention?

Admiral Smith: Give them more responsibility, more kinds of jobs where they are the boss, and paid attention to them, and have them come with their division at mast just as

---

* Acey-deucy is a variation of the board game backgammon.

the duty officer. All kinds of things—make them important. And speak to them, get to know them, talk to them.

Paul Stillwell: Did you walk around the ship and make yourself available to the crew?

Admiral Smith: Not to the crew, no. I think it's different today. No, I walked around the ship, and I was just a bit autocratic maybe, whatever. But we were run different in those days if you did it right. You can't play bosom pal with the crew. Not in my day you couldn't, and I don't think you can now. I think that's a mistake. Douglas Southall Freeman said leadership is know yourself, know your stuff, and take care of your men.[*] And you've got to know yourself; you've got to know whether you're the buddy-buddy type or whether you're going to be just a bit dignified. I think I had to be the latter. And so you know what you should do as a leader. Then you know your stuff, if you can, like handling that ship—whatever else is involved—and then take care of them.

Paul Stillwell: But they had gotten the word that they don't just walk up to you and start spilling their guts.

Admiral Smith: No, never. And even as a division officer, I never liked that. I remember in the *Arizona*, I was coming through the fifth division spaces before walking up onto the deck and coming up toward my division space. A couple sailors over in the fifth division came up and swearing and using filthy language. So I yelled at them and stopped them, "You knock off that stupid, filthy language, talk like a man," something like that, and went on up.

As I was coming up the ladder one of the sailors said, "That's the best son-of-a-bitch division officer on this ship." [Laughter] I didn't look back down at him either.

So you've got to be a little different, I think. There is a distinction.

---

[*] Douglas Southall Freeman, *Lee's Lieutenants: a Study in Command*, three volumes (New York: Scribner's, 1942-44).

Paul Stillwell: How was the relationship between you and Commander Peckham as far as dealing with the crew?

Admiral Smith: I think good. Now, Peckham was married in, I think, December of '49. I had him aboard and had the silver service broken out for him. I did all I could for Peckham, because he had had not a very happy first marriage, as I gather. I never inquired about it. But he was a fine officer, and I think his second marriage is perfectly great. They're getting along in years, both of them. He was a commander, of course.

I regret that the grounding of *Missouri* reflected on him, because he certainly was not at fault, in any way—no way.

Paul Stillwell: I found one more note I was going to ask you about. I saw in the log that drones had been used for target practice. How well did they work?

Admiral Smith: Very badly. They didn't work at all. They'd usually fall in before you hit them. No, drones weren't very good. Of course, they should be. You should get drones a much better target than the towed sleeve. Our modern gunnery just tears the sleeve apart. Like I told you about the British Far Eastern Fleet.

Paul Stillwell: Well, a drone could ideally be a lot more maneuverable.

Admiral Smith: Much more, much more. You probably have to get a larger drone that would behave more like an aircraft. That'd be terribly expensive. I don't know. I think you've simply got to run dry runs on aircraft and don't shoot anything, and depend on the missiles or gunnery, whatever else to do its stuff--direct practice and computer practices rather than actual firing. Loading the gun is easy enough; that's no problem.

Paul Stillwell: Did you have any practice using the big guns against sea targets, short-range and long-range battle practice?

Admiral Smith: No, and after World War II, you didn't have short-range practice any more; that was finished.

Paul Stillwell: And I made a note here that you had swim call a few times. Was that popular?

Admiral Smith: Right in the middle of the ocean? Yes, yes, they liked it. And then Admiral Smith loved it; he was a good swimmer. And he'd always get out there, and they'd have to take pictures of him, of course. Young midshipmen—we had boats out to start with. We put out boats with the rifles to be very sure that a shark didn't come along. But out in the middle of the ocean there aren't many sharks.

Paul Stillwell: Well, did you put lifeguards in the boats too?

Admiral Smith: Um-hm. They liked it. Calm day and everybody liked it. We put over nets that you could climb up on.

Paul Stillwell: I was just thinking about having two different periods in command. I would think that maybe the second would be anticlimactic in most cases. Was it that way for you, or did the mission make it different?

Admiral Smith: The mission made it entirely different. It was an entirely different cruise. There was so much that you had to do. I wasn't worried about the crew's confidence in me. I thought I probably had given them reason to have confidence in me on the first go-around. But I did have to make them get their confidence back again. But I trusted them and I believed in them, and so and so. And it worked; in time it worked. The officers of the deck became a little easier.

Paul Stillwell: Did you give Captain Duke any special briefings on what you'd been doing?

Admiral Smith: Oh, not a great deal. I don't think he wanted to hear—he didn't want to act like he was a beginner. But I told him of the differences in turning radius and things like this. He knew ship handling. I told him about the officers, what I thought of them, and if he had a possible problem, what it might be. And by that time I was pleased with the crew.

I asked him, I said, "Irv, you want to see the conning tower?"

"No, hell, I don't want to see that." Of course, he was an ordnance postgraduate. "No, I wouldn't understand that if you showed it to me." Irv was a good man. He's dead now.

Paul Stillwell: Well, now I think I really have come to the end of the questions. I thank you very much for your generous contribution here.

Admiral Smith: Well, sir, and can I get you anything refreshing before you go home?

Paul Stillwell: Well, I'd welcome that, thank you.

Admiral Smith: What would you like?

Interview Number 2 with Admiral Harold Page Smith, U.S. Navy (Retired)

Place: Admiral Smith's home in Virginia Beach, Virginia

Date: Friday, 26 October 1990

Paul Stillwell: Please tell me about your experiences in the *Arizona*.*

Admiral Smith: Well, I remember Captain Ward K. Wortman.† But the person who really interested me, I guess, was the gunnery officer, Pat Flanigan.‡ Pat was a rascal, black Irishman. He was a very attractive guy.

Paul Stillwell: A real wheeler-dealer later on in Europe.

Admiral Smith: He resigned or retired from the Navy after he made commander; he went on and became quite a wheel in business.

Paul Stillwell: He worked over in Europe for Admiral Stark during the war.§

Admiral Smith: Yes, he came back in, and I saw him once during the war. I was back in Admiral King's staff. King replaced Stark, you know, as CNO.** And Stark went on to London. I saw Pat Flanigan then. He was serious, as I remember him.

---

* USS *Arizona* (BB-39), a *Pennsylvania*-class battleship, was commissioned 17 October 1916. Originally she displaced 31,400 tons and was 608 feet long. She had a beam of 97 feet and a mean draft of 29 feet. Her top speed was 21 knots. She was armed with eight 14-inch guns, 22 5-inch guns, four 3-inch guns, and two 21-inch torpedo tubes. She was extensively modernized, 1929-31.
† Captain Ward K. Wortman, USN, commanded the battleship *Arizona* (BB-39) from 4 September 1928 to 29 April 1930.
‡ Lieutenant Commander Howard A. Flanigan, USN, had graduated from the Naval Academy in the class of 1910. Flanigan retired as a commander in 1936 and subsequently worked on the New York World's Fair of 1939-40. He was recalled to active duty from 15 May 1941 to 3 February 1946, eventually being promoted to rear admiral on the retired list.
§ Admiral Harold R. Stark, USN, served as Commander U.S. Naval Forces Europe from 30 April 1942 to 15 August 1945.
** Admiral Ernest J. King, USN, served as Chief of Naval Operations from 26 March 1942 to 15 December 1945 and as Commander in Chief U.S. Fleet from 20 December 1941 to 2 September 1945; he was promoted to the rank of fleet admiral in December 1944.

Arleigh Burke and I swapped jobs.* At least I came to the *Arizona*, and he went on to the *Procyon*, where I was. Arleigh had been assistant plotting room officer, I think was his title, and I didn't want that job. I wanted a turret. I appealed to the gunnery officer, Flanigan, to give me a turret. He didn't think I knew anything. He didn't like the whole idea, but he had a turret. A classmate of mine named Jinx Longfellow just had the turret, and he'd been sent off to a destroyer.† His turret had failed in his last gunnery practice—short-range battle practice. Made a low score. So he gave me that turret, and I worked real hard on it too. I'd never had a turret job before. But I remember the day of short-range battle practice. I'd been aboard the ship about a month. I'd worked real hard, too, to get ready for it. Pat came in to make his final inspection of the turret, and he said to Lieutenant George Kraker, who was his plotting room officer, "I'm worried about this turret."‡ Well, I was worried already myself, but we got an E.§

Paul Stillwell: Why were you worried?

Admiral Smith: I was worried as hell that something would go wrong. And he was so concerned because I'd never fired a turret; I'd never been turret officer. I'd never been in the turret, actually. But I knew all about this turret, worked with the men and tried to teach them and train them and so and so.

Paul Stillwell: You remember a ceremony for handing out prize money?

Admiral Smith: Fifteen dollars for each man, yes. [Chuckle] That was lots of fun.

The other turret officers, each one of them was more experienced than I, of course, and had been through more training period than I.

---

* Lieutenant (junior grade) Arleigh A. Burke, USN, served on board the *Arizona* from his graduation in 1923 until 1928. He was later Chief of Naval Operations from 1955 to 1961.
† Lieutenant (junior grade) William J. Longfellow, USN.
‡ Lieutenant George Patton Kraker, USN.
§ An "E," for excellence, is generally awarded to a ship or component of a ship as a result of top performance in competition with other ships during a given time period.

Let's see, turret two was McDill, jaygee; and turret three was Joe Daniel; and turret four was Tee Benson.*

Paul Stillwell: I've got a list of the officers from that time, if that would help refresh your memory.

Admiral Smith: I remember those guys. I remember that they all ran their turrets, satisfactory, but I none of them got E's. Ward K. Wortman, yes. They were friends. I remember my friends fondly, old Pat Flanigan. Wellbrock, hell of a good man, too, very good.† Woodruff engineer, little bitty man. Funny thing about [goes through list of names] Derx, Rockwell, Sample, George Dyer, Gregg, Louis Corman, Kraker, and Harry Corman—two Corman boys—Jewish officers, both of them.‡ Class of '22, as I remember, those people. And one of the Corman boys, I remember, told a story I'll never forget. Right after his graduation, he had been in a destroyer in the port of Smyrna in Turkey, where the Greeks were being run off by the Turks.

Paul Stillwell: The *Arizona* was over there about that time.

Admiral Smith: He was in a destroyer then, and he recalled he'd wake up with nightmares. He recalled the Greeks trying to crawl aboard this destroyer—near the border. He had stopped taking any people on board, because he was afraid the ship might capsize. There were so damn many of them. He said, "As we steamed out of Smyrna, [Izmir, they call it now] just loaded down and pushed the people off to die." I remember Harry Corman telling me that.

---

* Lieutenant (junior grade) Alexander S. McDill, USN; Lieutenant (junior grade) John C. Daniel, USN; Lieutenant (junior grade) William H. Benson, USN.
† Lieutenant Commander John H. Wellbrock, USN, navigator. Lieutenant Commander George L. Woodruff, USN, engineer officer.
‡ Lieutenant M. R. Derx, USN; Lieutenant C. R. Rockwell, USN; Lieutenant George C. Dyer, USN; Lieutenant W. H. Gregg, USN; Lieutenant Louis Corman, USN; Lieutenant George P. Kraker, USN; Lieutenant H. Corman, USN.

Paul Stillwell: Do you remember Captain Tarrant?*

Admiral Smith: Tarrant came on, yes, and he was succeeded by Kimberly.†

Paul Stillwell: Well, he was before Wortman.

Admiral Smith: Yes, of course he was. Wait a minute. I thought Tarrant came after Wortman.

Paul Stillwell: No, Wortman was the officer who took her around into the navy yard for the modernization . . .

Admiral Smith: Yes, of course.

Paul Stillwell: . . . and there was one officer in there for just a brief time in between called Kimberly. He went to take command of the *Maryland* after he'd been in the Arizona only a few months, and that seemed like an odd circumstance, just reading it in the log.

Admiral Smith: Yes, *Maryland* was a superior ship, of course, but he had some friends and maybe they gave him a better job.

Paul Stillwell: Maybe so.

Admiral Smith: Tarrant, I remember well. The last time I saw him was in Washington when I was—I wanted something to add there. He was, of course, an old man then and retired. I went to some reception, and he was sitting in the corner of the room with some other old men. I didn't think he'd know me, so I walked over to him and introduced

---

* Captain William T. Tarrant, USN, commanded the USS *Arizona* (BB-39) from 24 May 1927 to 27 June 1928. He later retired on 1 August 1942 as a vice admiral.
† Captain Victor A. Kimberly, USN, commanded the *Arizona* (BB-39) from 27 June 1928 to 4 September 1928.

myself. He said, "I was just wondering how long it was going to take you to come over and say hello." [Laughter] Very attractive old man.

Paul Stillwell: It's interesting, because in the photos I've seen, he looks like a very austere person.

Admiral Smith: No, he had a sense of humor. I do remember that he had only been aboard a short time, and we went north in the *Arizona*. I remember I had the deck, and he came on the bridge. It was a foggy morning, and out of the fog came a division of cruisers with a rear admiral. So, of course, you immediately saluted that rear admiral. I sounded the word to man the saluting battery. And word came back up that the warrant gunner was in the shower. So the captain said, "You go down and fire the salute." I had never fired a salute, but I went down and fired the salute: "If I wasn't a gunner, I wouldn't be here. Fire. If I wasn't a gunner, I wouldn't be here."[*]

I came back up, you know, and said, "Sir, I fired a 13-gun, sir."

He said, "That's the best salute I've heard fired out here in the sea."

"I thank you, sir." That's the first one he'd heard fired. [Laughter] He was waiting to see if I caught on, how long it took me, how sharp I was.

No, he was a very attractive man.

Ward K. Wortman was quite a different man, but in his way, very attractive too. But he was a rascal.

Paul Stillwell: George Dyer talked about Wortman in his oral history.[†] And he didn't have too many kind things to say about him.

Admiral Smith: Well, I'll give you one of the good ones.

I do remember one thing I'll never forget about Ward K. Wortman. In Guantánamo Bay, Cuba—that's when we came around to turn her in to the shipyard here

---

[*] The interval between shots fired by saluting batteries is five seconds. Thus the warrant gunner or other person in charge timed the interval by repeating a chant, "If I wasn't a gunner, I wouldn't be here. Fire. If I wasn't a gunner, I wouldn't be here. Fire."

[†] See the Naval Institute oral history of Vice Admiral George C. Dyer, USN (Ret.).

in Norfolk. One morning in Guantánamo Bay, why, the word was passed for a coxswain in my division—Hendricks—never forget his name. Hendricks was the gig coxswain, and he was on report.* And the division officer always went to mast with members of his division. I said, "What did you do, Hendricks?"

He said, "Nothing. I don't know anything, Lieutenant."

So Ward K. Wortman held mast, and he pronounced sentence on everybody there until Hendricks. Everybody else was gone, and he said, "Hendricks, you embarrassed me last night. When you brought the gig alongside the gangway here at *Arizona,* you rammed it two or three times. I had trouble getting . . ."

Hendricks said, "Captain, I didn't bring you back last night; you came back with the captain from *Tennessee.*"

Wortman said, "Case dismissed." [Chuckle]

He was a rascal, but I got along with him fine.

Paul Stillwell: What do you remember about handling the ship in formation?

Admiral Smith: Oh, she was like a big old tub; she was easy enough. I was a good watch officer—at least I was regarded as such. And, boy, she was slow. It was easy enough if you knew how to handle, what to do, and way it turned. But she was very slow.

Paul Stillwell: So you have to anticipate.

Admiral Smith: Yes, you have to think about it. But nothing, of course, like *Missouri*. *Missouri* was like a destroyer.

Paul Stillwell: Well, she didn't have nearly the power.

Admiral Smith: No, I saw her at full power a couple times, I guess, during my time aboard. She'd groan and grunt and finally make 20 knots with smoke pouring out and so.

---

* Gig is the name for the boat assigned to the commanding officer of a Navy ship.

Paul Stillwell: Well, she had only 30-some thousand horsepower compared to 212,000.

Admiral Smith: That's right. But you really had to think about how slow she was when she was making the turns and so. You had standard 15 degrees rudder to make such a turn. With all the battleships, if you were following in column, why, all the battleships did the same thing, so it wasn't too difficult.

With Ward K. Wortman I was one of four watch officers. I think he was the one that let only four of have the deck, and I was by that time experienced. I came aboard the *Arizona* in April of '28.

Paul Stillwell: In San Francisco.

Admiral Smith: Yes, and then I finally went around to Norfolk and transferred in July of '29. Transferred to *Nevada*—brought her out. I do remember leaving the *Arizona*. I was going to go to turret one in the *Nevada*. I'd been assured of that by talking to the executive officer over there, Commander Cake in *Nevada*.[*] He promised me turret one, so I took my best crew out of the *Arizona*, of course.[†] Sure enough, after a short time, why, we were to have short-range battle practice. And just a couple weeks before short-range battle practice, the gunnery officer made me transfer one of my pointer crews—you had two pointer crews—the pointer trainer and the firing pointer—two crews. Each one of them in short-range battle practice would fire three salvos. And I had to transfer one set of pointers to the turret two. And I had to train another set, but I still put an E on that turret two. That was fun. Those are the kinds of things you remember.

Paul Stillwell: Well, it's an interesting challenge.

Admiral Smith: Yes.

---

[*] Commander Stuart W. Cake, USN.
[†] The battleship *Nevada* (BB-36) was just coming out of a long modernization overhaul and thus building up the crew. The crew of the *Arizona* was reduced in preparation for her being out of service during modernization.

Paul Stillwell: I interviewed, the other night, an enlisted man who made that same transition you did. He came around to the East Coast in the *Arizona* and then went to the *Nevada*. He remembered the beginning of the process of the dismantling of the topsides in the *Arizona*.

Admiral Smith: I didn't see that. We pulled out and went on down to Guantánamo for gunnery training, shakedown on the ship, and so on and so on and so on.

Paul Stillwell: He said that the tops came off first, and then gradually sections of the cage mast.

Admiral Smith: Yes. She ended up with tripods.

Paul Stillwell: Right.
    He also said that Captain Wortman brought a parrot around to the East Coast on board this ship.

Admiral Smith: I don't remember that.

Paul Stillwell: He said the Marine orderlies taught it some foul language while they were standing watches outside his cabin.

Admiral Smith: That was standard procedure.
    I remember in the old *Procyon*, we put into Corinto, Nicaragua, to bring out a company of Marines and their officers. And with them was a young chaplain, Marine lieutenant, and he had a parrot. And we tried desperately to make that parrot learn some good language. But he just looked at you, refused to talk at all. [Laughter]

Paul Stillwell: One enlisted man from that era said that a number of the ship's Marines were taken off and sent into Nicaragua, with the result that some of the normal Marine duties were performed by sailors.

Admiral Smith: That I wouldn't remember; I don't remember that.

Paul Stillwell: Maybe that was earlier or later—I don't remember that, no.

Admiral Smith: We didn't go into Nicaragua in my tour, no.

Paul Stillwell: Still another recollection, one enlisted man said that there was a bathtub for senior officers in the *Arizona*. Do you recall that?

Admiral Smith: Yes. For President Hoover.[*]

Paul Stillwell: This would have been even before that, apparently.
His story was that . . .

Admiral Smith: I never saw it, I don't think. But I remember there was a bathtub, I think, put in the captain's cabin. It just strikes some memory of mine. I don't think I ever saw it.

Paul Stillwell: He sort of told it like it was for department heads. And in his recollection, his job was to clean the head, and one time he went in there and took a bath himself and forgot to lock the door behind him. And I don't know how plausible that story is.

Admiral Smith: I doubt that. I don't know. I was a wardroom officer, and I don't believe there was any such thing as that. If there had been a bathtub, it'd be either in the captain's cabin or the executive officer's cabin. It wouldn't have been for heads of departments, no, because the wardroom officers were to use the same toilets and baths.

Paul Stillwell: That's one of those stories that's too good to be true, I guess.

---

[*] President Herbert C. Hoover spent time on board the *Arizona* during a cruise in 1931, but the bathtub must have been there earlier as well, because Smith left in 1939.

Admiral Smith: Yes, I'm afraid so. [Chuckle]

Paul Stillwell: Well, what recollections do you have in running the wardroom mess?

Admiral Smith: I recall it being a very, very happy mess. When I first came aboard, I remember playing bridge with the people there. We didn't have any serious poker games. I do remember that executive officer frowned on heavy gambling. We played bridge, and I remember very good bridge players aboard, those kinds of games.

There was a young doctor who later became a rear admiral in the Medical Corps. Gordon I believe is his name.* And his predecessor, the captain medical officer on the *Arizona* transferred and became the executive officer over at Portsmouth. I think when we came around and he transferred over there. He was promoted to captain. And I remember this doctor saying—what the hell was his name?—saying he hated to go to the hospital because he said, "I'm a neurologist. When I get over to the hospital, I'll be just a manager. I don't like that."†

Paul Stillwell: Was that almost a nightly thing, the bridge game?

Admiral Smith: Pretty much, yes. Or even in port if you had the day's duty. Yes, you'd have a bridge game. It was rather a relaxed life, not nearly with the kind of anxiety you have today, like the Persian Gulf crisis, or like the wartime, no.‡ Much more relaxed.

Paul Stillwell: I was just reading the article about when President Hoover came aboard in '31, that somebody from RCA set up the *Arizona* as the first Navy ship to have a sound movie projector, because sound movies were new then and that was the novelty. Did you have silent movies in the *Arizona*?

---

* Lieutenant (junior grade) John N. C. Gordon, Medical Corps, USN.
† Commander Harry A. Garrison, Medical Corps, USN, was the senior doctor on board the *Arizona*.
‡ In January 1991 U.S. and Allied Coalition forces attacked Iraq to get it to retreat following its August 1990 invasion of neighboring Kuwait. The holding action in the meantime was Operation Desert Shield. The conflict itself became known variously as Operation Desert Storm and the Gulf War. Coalition forces won the war in February 1991.

Admiral Smith: I think we had silent movies when I was aboard; yes, I'm sure we did.

Paul Stillwell: What other forms of recreation do you recall?

Admiral Smith: Oh, there was some effort at badminton, but not very much. Nobody cared very much for that. I remember a new executive officer, just before I left, I think, and he insisted everybody have a basketball team. I had to pick a basketball team to try to—but nobody cared much for it even, didn't like it. Wasn't any place, you know—you could throw a ball into a hoop, but there was no place to have a gymnasium and you have to go ashore to do that, so that wasn't very much fun.

Paul Stillwell: What emphasis do you remember on safety in the turrets? And this was not too long after the *Mississippi* explosion.*

Admiral Smith: That was so simple, so easy. The turret is the safest place on the ship, literally. So simple. And if you're careful with your safety precautions and you worked up gradually at speed—you practice every day, you know. Every morning you had turret practice. And you practiced with dummy drill bags and dummy projectile—ram the projectile, then have a backing-out slug that weighed 500 pounds and drop this slug back down the elevated gun and knock the bullet out and go through the process again.

I remember winning a dollar on that backing-out slug. It weighed 500 pounds. And we had one turret captain, gunner's mate, named Pryzbilski. Now I remember some names—Pryzbilski. He was a powerful man, and he could just reach down and strain, but he'd pick up 500 pounds. I said, "I can pick that thing up. I can lift it off the deck at least." And, hell, we bet a dollar. I put a bar across my knees, through the eye in the backing-out slug, raise up my heels, and lifted it up. He said it wasn't fair—I raised—I lifted it. So he had to pay me a dollar, which I think I paid him back. [Chuckle]

---

* While the battleship *Mississippi* (BB-41) was engaged in gunnery practice on 12 June 1924, turret two exploded, killing 48 men.

He was also on my rifle team. I was a fairly good rifleman. I was a little better than expert. And so I had to involve myself in the drilling of the rifle team. I was one of the two—Clarence Coffin and I were the two officers on our ship's rifle team.*

Paul Stillwell: I talked to him last year.

Admiral Smith: Clarence Coffin?

Paul Stillwell: Yes, sir.

Admiral Smith: He was good; he was very good, very good. He'd won the President's rifle at Camp Perry rifle shooting. I was invited to go once, but I realized that going out to Camp Perry, you gave up an awful lot of other things, and probably give up a career of getting on to other jobs. So you'd be too likely to make a career out of rifle shooting. Had one classmate who did and failed at his future promotions. But among other things, I did have the occasion to train a company of the bluejacket landing force.

Another little anecdote about the *Arizona*. The state of Arizona gave us a pit bulldog puppy. There are three different shades of color of the pit bulls. There's white, and there's black and white, and there's a brindle. And Arizona gave us an Arizona brindle. I think they bred them out there. He was a beautiful pup, of course, and we had one little, bitty dog—fox terrier, I think. He was a mascot aboard the ship. And this big bull pup played with the little dog; he was very happy. We took him ashore, training the landing force once, and up came a big airedale and jumped the pit bull. He was fairly well grown, just still a pup, but he jumped him. And the pit bull was astonished and surprised, but he killed the airedale. We tried to beat him off the dog with butts, but he killed him. Then we had to be very careful of him, because he became a killer.

Paul Stillwell: Well, that breed is known for that.

---

* Ensign Clarence E. Coffin Jr., USN.

Admiral Smith: Yes, that was his job, and he realized that's what he had to do. So I was very sad that we had to kill him. Put him to sleep, I think you say.

Paul Stillwell: I'd be interested in more of that backing-out slug, just how you used that.

Admiral Smith: Very simple. As you know, first—with the turret gun level, why, you ram the projectile in. The rammer is withdrawn, the doors open, powder bags are put on, and the rammer slowly pushes these bags in.

Paul Stillwell: Four bags?

Admiral Smith: Four bags, yes. *Missouri* had either five or six. Six, I think, was a full load. And you could drill with five, but six was a full load.

And then the rammer was drawn and the gun captain, plug man, closed the breech, tightened up, the primer was inserted and BAM! You fired when you were ready, which was so simple and so—you couldn't do any one of these processes—you couldn't open the powder room door until you had rammed the shell and withdrawn the rammer. Then the powder room door opened, and the tray came out and these bags rolled in, and the rammer man pushed them in slowly. You trained, trained, trained at that until it was letter perfect, which makes me wonder about the *Iowa* thing.[*] From all accounts, the rammer man was new that previous day. It was his first day ramming in that turret, as I read the news . . .

Paul Stillwell: I'm not sure on that.

Admiral Smith: Well, it was so stupid, you can't believe it. There were men in responsible positions in that turret that had only been there a short time and transferred from another turret or something. So I can't believe that that turret was well trained. And I do think, without a question, that the accident was caused by the rammer man.

---

[*] On 19 April 1989, an explosion occurred in the center gun of turret two on board the USS *Iowa* (BB-61) during firing operations off Puerto Rico. As a result of the accident, 47 of her crew members were killed.

Paul Stillwell: Well, but he was being directed by this guy that's been accused of killing people.*

Admiral Smith: Well, the gun captain—now there, again, because this man had some accusations—he was new too.

Paul Stillwell: Yes.

Admiral Smith: It's unbelievable. I can't believe it. Of course, we had really trained an awful lot by the time we ever fired a gun.

Paul Stillwell: Well, on these occasions when you didn't fire, was the gun in the loading position, when you used the backing-out slug?

Admiral Smith: Oh, no, no. After you rammed, then you elevated the gun to whatever you were aiming at. Maybe a short-range battle practice just a tiny bit, just a few degrees. But for long-range battle practice, elevated 15 degrees. And then when that was completed, why, you lowered the gun, inserted the backing-out slug—the gun being level.

Paul Stillwell: You'd have to put in the muzzle.

Admiral Smith: Put in the muzzle, and the gun elevated and then you turned loose of the rope that was holding it.

Paul Stillwell: Oh, I see, just by momentum, it . . .

---

* The Navy's initial investigation of the turret explosion on board the *Iowa* found that Gunner's Mate Third Class Clayton Hartwig had killed himself and his shipmates by placing a device in the breech of a 16-inch gun. Subsequent tests determined that the explosion could have been caused by over-ramming of powder bags into the gun, and the Navy withdrew its claims that Hartwig had been responsible.

Admiral Smith: Yes, just turn loose the rope that you're holding it with, let it turn loose, and she'd bound into the projectile and knock it out.

Paul Stillwell: Then you'd send it back down to the . . .

Admiral Smith: Normally, yes, you'd put it back in. Go through the whole procedure, put it back down in the handling room—upper shell handling room.

Paul Stillwell: What was the purpose of those little sub-caliber barrels that were on top of the 14-inch guns? They looked almost like the telescopic sight for a rifle.

Admiral Smith: I can't remember what we did with those. I know we didn't use them in any way in the sighting or laying of the guns. Never used them. I can't remember what we used them for. That's a blank in my mind.

Paul Stillwell: That's one thing I just haven't been able to find out yet. I've seen pictures of them on a number of occasions.

Admiral Smith: Damn if I think we had one on my turret.

Paul Stillwell: I got the impression they were things that you could remove.

Admiral Smith: Was it a machine gun?

Paul Stillwell: No, it wasn't a machine gun. It looked a lot like a gun sight. Just a little telescopic thing.

Admiral Smith: Would you introduce it in the—no way in the turret, had nothing to do with the turret firing, because your sights in the turret were down just before the end of the turret.

And the pointer in the left side, in the firing pointer and the trainer. The trainer handled the controls in this direction, left and right. And the firing pointer was the guy who fired when he felt they were all on target at short-range battle practice.

For a long-range battle practice, of course, you elevated the guns as directed by the plotting room for the range selected. And that could be done electrically, or you could have people match pointers and bring them up as you desired.

Paul Stillwell: Oh, so you actually had a kind of remote control, servo type.

Admiral Smith: Yes, you could do it from the plotting room, or you could have them match pointers, as we called it.

Paul Stillwell: Was that plotting room down on the third deck of . . .

Admiral Smith: Yes, it was down in the center of the ship.

Paul Stillwell: But I take it there was just one plotting room, whereas, the *Iowa* and the *Missouri* had two, forward and aft both.

Admiral Smith: Yes, the *Arizona* had the one—the single plotting room, yes.

Paul Stillwell: What was the connection between the directors all the way up in the tops and the plotting room?

Admiral Smith: The directors in the tops, you had a spotter, we called him. And he was an officer of some experience. And with this telescope he would see whether or not the shell landed short or over, you know—right or left. And he would spot them down 500, left 200 or something of that sort.

Paul Stillwell: Of course, he didn't have a range finder up there.

Admiral Smith: No, range finders were mounted on the turrets. On the *Arizona*, they were on the turret two and turret three. My Lord, I can't even remember those ships.

But the spotters, you had one in the foretop and another one in the main top. He was assisted, of course, but he would collaborate.

Paul Stillwell: And then there were those little houses partway up the masts, I guess were used for spotting on the secondary battery. These structures here [pointing to photo].

Admiral Smith: Yes, that's right.

Paul Stillwell: How much were the airplanes used for spotting?

Admiral Smith: They were used quite a bit for spotting; they were very good too.

In long-range battle practice, the aircraft spotter was the primary spotter. And his estimates of distance were used, preferably to the foretop spotter.

Paul Stillwell: What would that be, maybe 15,000-20,000 yards?

Admiral Smith: My heavens, let me see now. You know, I've forgotten the range of those things. I know the 5-inch guns' range was about 15,000 yards. The turret guns were about 25,000 or so.

Paul Stillwell: Would the long-range battle practice be held out at the maximum range?

Admiral Smith: Yes, yes. Or close to it.

Paul Stillwell: What do you remember about the operation of the planes around the ship? Were they recovered under way?

Admiral Smith: Oh, yes. The battleship under way would make a turn, so it would make a slick. And the plane would come in and land and cruise up into the slick as the battleship would keep on turning under a crane and hook onto the plane and hook it up. You would do that, especially if there was any kind of sea. You wouldn't use it in a very rough sea, of course. But with even a moderate sea, why, you could make quite a slick with turning the ship.

Paul Stillwell: There was kind of a boom all the way at the stern. Was that used to pick the planes up?

Admiral Smith: Yes. That boom with the stern, also, if you didn't catapult, you could lower him away, let him take off there.

Paul Stillwell: Was that done sometimes?

Admiral Smith: Yes, sometimes, yes.

Paul Stillwell: I have read that that was the pneumatic-type catapult, and later she got the one with the powder charge.

Admiral Smith: The first ones I remember were pneumatic, and then, of course, later the powder charges. I don't ever remember seeing an accident, either, with the floatplanes.

Paul Stillwell: I talked to old Admiral Pride, who was later Chief of the Bureau of Aeronautics.*

Admiral Smith: Mel Pride.

Paul Stillwell: Right. He was a pilot in the *Arizona* in 1920.

Admiral Smith: Mel Pride's not alive yet, is he?

---

* Rear Admiral Alfred M. Pride, USN, served as Chief of the Bureau of Aeronautics from 1 May 1947 to 1 May 1951. His oral history is in the Naval Institute collection.

Paul Stillwell: No, he died a couple years ago.

Admiral Smith: I was quite certain of that, yes.

Paul Stillwell: But there weren't even catapults yet. There were just wooden platforms on the tops of the high turrets, and so he had to land ashore. There was no float on the plane either.

Admiral Smith: Yes, that's right. That's right.

Paul Stillwell: He showed me a picture of himself with a mule hooked up to his airplane in Cuba, so they could take it down to the water's edge and bring it back out to the ship by boat.

Admiral Smith: That's before my time. I don't remember one of those kinds of things. I do remember, though, how useful those floatplanes were.

In January of 1945, I had my squadron of destroyers with a cruiser division. We went up to harass the Japanese in Iwo Jima and up to Chichi Jima, just chewed up the works and sank any ships we found. As we came in toward Iwo Jima just before dawn, a cruiser launched a plane. And the plane reported after a few minutes that there was a Japanese cruiser anchored off the east coast of Iwo Jima. And our cruiser rear admiral ordered me to send in two destroyers to sink the cruiser. So I took my flag boat, the *Dunlap*, and the *Fanning*, and off we went, smoking. We wanted to get in there before he could see us. And as luck would have it, here's where I know about the raid, because at 15,000 and a few yards, we opened fire, and both destroyers hit on the first salvo.* And the Jap never got off a shot.

Later on, when I was the duke of the Iwo Jima up there, after we took Iwo Jima, they left me there with my squadron, why, I went over to see it. They managed to beach the ship, but it was all full of holes. We really worked it over.

---

* On 24 January 1945 the *Dunlap* (DD-384) and the *Fanning* (DD-385) sank three small Japanese cargo ships near Iwo Jima in the Bonin Islands. On 19 June the *Duncan* sank an enemy surface craft that was trying to evacuate personnel from Chichi Jima. The *Duncan* rescued 52 survivors.

Paul Stillwell: So you got it with guns before you got into torpedo range.

Admiral Smith: Oh, yes, I intended to hit him as early as we could. We were going to fire torpedoes, but didn't have to because—wonderful—of course, we had radar then—beautiful radar. And those ships hit on the first salvo, both of them. You wouldn't believe it.

Paul Stillwell: What do you recall about operating the *Arizona* in fog with no radar?

Admiral Smith: Worrisome, really worrisome. And you slowed too. You didn't proceed at any great speed. You slowed to five knots if you were in fog. And you got out on the wing of the bridge and strained your eyes too. You were better without using glasses. You could see better without binoculars. And you put lookouts in the bows of the ship too. Tell you what they saw.

Paul Stillwell: Did you have any flag officers on board during your time in the *Arizona*?

Admiral Smith: If so, just temporarily, because the *Pennsylvania* was the flagship of our division. *Pennsylvania* and *Arizona* were sisters. And we usually had the *New Mexico* with us for some reason or other; she made the third ship of the division. I don't know why that was back in my day, because the *New Mexico*, *Idaho*, and *Mississippi* were the three sisters.

Paul Stillwell: Later they were put back into their own division.

Admiral Smith: Yes, yes. And *Utah* was another old one. My memory is real weak about that ship now.

Paul Stillwell: I wouldn't say so.

    The *Arizona* was a flagship during much of the '30s. She got a good flag setup when she came back out of the yard.

Admiral Smith: Yes, when she'd been modernized. Guns elevated to 30 degrees instead of the 15 she had been. And she had blisters.* I was familiar with the blisters, though, in *Nevada*. She had the same modernization, because I remember going through Panama Canal. Paddy Hyland was our first captain in *Nevada*.†

Paul Stillwell: John Hyland's dad.‡

Admiral Smith: Yes. He was the captain at one time or the other. At any rate, going through the Panama Canal, the pilot misjudged the turn. Of course, she was awfully clumsy with—both ships had to be clumsy. And he nudged the mud bank making the turn into the canal. And the skipper told me to go down, and my division, of course, first division, had the starboard side. I had to go down and inspect each one of those double bottoms in Panama, where the temperature was—Lord, I came out weighing at least ten pounds less after I had finished. But no damage was done. The ship just barely rubbed the mud, and off it went.

Paul Stillwell: What do you recall about the Marines in the *Arizona*?

Admiral Smith: Marines—very little, except they were an excellent outfit. We never had anything except topnotch Marines. And they were an excellent outfit. I do remember in the *Nevada* that with my assembly of the best men that we had in the *Arizona*, turret one, my division in the *Nevada* beat the Marines in rifle firing. My team of eight persons, me and one other officer, too, beat the Marines and two officers. And I do remember the Marine captain was found searching through the records in the executive's office—personnel office—to see if all my men were legal. First time any Marine detachment ever was beaten by a Navy crew.

---

* When the old battleships were modernized, external compartments were welded onto the ships' hulls at the waterline to provide increased protection against torpedo damage. The compartments were nicknamed "blisters."
† Captain John J. Hyland, USN, commanded the battleship *Nevada* (BB-36) from 12 July 1930 to 30 April 1932.
‡ Admiral John J. Hyland Jr., USN, served as Commander in Chief Pacific Fleet from 30 November 1967 to 5 December 1970. His oral history is in the Naval Institute collection.

Paul Stillwell: How could they be illegal? Where did he think you got them?

Admiral Smith: Transferred too soon or borrowed from another division. Mine were all legal.

Paul Stillwell: Oh, I see. What do you remember about the operation of the ship's boats?

Admiral Smith: Nothing particular comes to mind, except my story about Hendricks and the captain's gig. Why do I remember that boy's name? He was a good gig captain.

Paul Stillwell: This enlisted man I talked to the other night was a boat engineer in the A division. And he said they had gasoline-powered motor launches, and they really had to be careful about the fire hazard.

Admiral Smith: Yes, there were—I don't remember ever seeing a fire in the boat. I do remember that they'd fail you. I don't remember any failure or embarrassing one in *Arizona*.

I do remember in *Idaho*, one unhappy memory comes to mind. I was a junior officer in the *Idaho*. On the morning watch, 6:00 o'clock, something of that sort, the officer of the deck—senior to me, of course—had called away the captain's gig running around the ship a couple times. Captain Crosley was going ashore at, say, 6:15 or something to meet a train or something.[*]

And then just to be damn sure, the officer of the deck got a motorboat running around. And then the motorboat quit. So then he got a motor launch, and it'd run around and keep running. And then he called away the captain's gig again. And the captain's gig wouldn't run. So the captain had to go ashore—the number-one motor launch was alongside the ship, a 50-footer. The officer of the deck said, "Captain, I'm very sorry, but the gig is not operating." And he said, "I'm sorry, but we have number-one motor launch."

---

[*] Captain Walter S. Crosley, USN.

And the captain said, "Very well, Lieutenant, turn over the deck to your relief. Then report to your room for six to ten days under arrest for ten days."

Paul Stillwell: Do you remember officers in the *Arizona* being put in hack like that?

Admiral Smith: No, I don't remember. In my time only once I put an officer—twice I put an officer under suspension, arrest for ten days.

Paul Stillwell: But I think it was much more commonly done then than now.

Admiral Smith: Oh, yes. I don't know why not. It was a very salubrious undertaking.

My first young officer to be put under suspension was because he almost missed his ship coming—well, he missed getting back to his ship by some three hours—but fortunate to get back before we sailed out in China. So I put him under suspension for ten days.

Paul Stillwell: Was that when you commanded the *Stewart*?

Admiral Smith: Yes. And he never took another drink, not in my time . . .

Paul Stillwell: You got his attention.

Admiral Smith: And apparently he didn't resent it, because I do remember this young officer—he left the ship before war came on. But after the war, sometime or other, I was back in Washington, and he was then a captain and invited my wife and me to dinner. He made the first invitation. So he'd forgiven me, whatever injury I did to his pride at the time.

But I think it saved that officer. That reminds me of the—you know, everybody remembers that Patton slapped a soldier.[*] But they don't remember that that slapped

---

[*] In August 1943, while in command of the Sicily campaign, Lieutenant General George S. Patton, USA, slapped two soldiers who were suffering from battle fatigue because he thought they were malingering.

soldier, furious, went back to his outfit as ordered, became a good soldier, and in Germany was given a medal.

Paul Stillwell: I didn't know that.

Admiral Smith: Yes. That's the kind of thing I remember. Another end to the story.
So Patton saved the soldier.
I don't think I've given you much information of any use to you.

Paul Stillwell: Yes, sir, you have. Still are.
What do you remember about Long Beach-San Pedro as a homeport for the *Arizona*?

Admiral Smith: Well, the times were quiet. They were comfortable places. There was no violence of any sort that you could remember. There were certainly no drugs, and any drinking was rather quietly handled. No crime of any sort.

Paul Stillwell: Prohibition was still in effect, so it had to be quiet.[*]

Admiral Smith: It was quiet but—oh, there was drinking but then it was done quietly—ashore, of course. I never saw drinking aboard ship.

Paul Stillwell: How were the supplies of alcohol gotten?

Admiral Smith: They were pretty carefully taken care of, I guess. I never saw any—I'm not aware of any case where alcohol was drunk. Of course, the alcohol for the compasses, you know, had to be carefully cared for. A sailor would drink that if he got his hand on it, maybe. I don't remember seeing any kind of punishment meted out for

---

[*] The 18th Amendment to the Constitution was ratified in 1919 and went into effect in 1920, prohibiting the consumption of alcoholic beverages in the United States. The Volstead Act, enacted by Congress in 1919, spelled out the penalties for violations. In December 1933 the ratification of the 21st Amendment to the Constitution repealed the 18th Amendment and thus ended national prohibition.

crime aboard ship. None. We didn't have crime. Fights, yes, sure, but—a sailor would fight sometimes but then . . .

Paul Stillwell: Sometimes I think the torpedo alcohol was appropriated also.

Admiral Smith: Probably, but—of course, *Arizona* back in the old days had torpedoes, you know.

Paul Stillwell: Did she fire those while you were on board?

Admiral Smith: Yes.

Paul Stillwell: How was a torpedo practice run?

Admiral Smith: Like for a destroyer. Of course, you had to put target boats out and watch—be sure the torpedo passed under the target boats. As I recall, we put three boats out, and one of them towing the other two so to keep the lines—keep a little speed on the boats. And a mast in the center one, and the torpedo would fire. Then you'd observe whether it passed under or not. I never had any part of the torpedo firing, although I do remember being in a boat some time or another.

Paul Stillwell: Well, when you've got guns that have much longer range, it's not a very realistic tactic.

Admiral Smith: It wasn't realistic, and, of course, they were abandoned later on.

Paul Stillwell: Well, as soon as she went into the yard, as a matter of fact.

Admiral Smith: Yes. They had to come off when the blisters were put on.

Paul Stillwell: Well, it made good sense.

Admiral Smith: Yes. But we used very, very few torpedoes in World War II. I do remember when I was a budget officer in the Navy, back in 1955-56, that I discovered among—you know, a budget officer's supposed to try to find some way to save money, so if you buy something new—I discovered that we were keeping in maintenance something like five times the number of torpedoes we fired in World War II. So I managed to get rid of an awful lot of torpedoes and get them scrapped and save all that money and time. Same way I was able during my time, and as budget officer, to bring about the scrapping of the *California* and *Tennessee*, the last two 14-inch battleships.* And the maintenance of those two ships, with the enormous amount of spares and ammunition that was kept ready for them, probably never be used again, was so silly that we kept them that long. This, of course, after World War II that I was able to get them scrapped.

Paul Stillwell: Yes, they hung around for quite a while.

Admiral Smith: Yes. We saved an awful lot of ships for a long while. We kept the *Alabama* and *Massachusetts* and *North Carolina* for quite a while. Finally got rid of them.

Paul Stillwell: Those didn't go till the early '60s.

Admiral Smith: Quite a long time. I think the *Alabama* wasn't given away to the state of Alabama until 1963.†

Paul Stillwell: Right about then, yes, sir.

---

* The *California* (BB-44) and *Tennessee* (BB-43) were sold for scrap 10 July 1959 after being in mothballs since their decommissioning in 1947.
† The decommissioned battleship *Alabama* (BB-60) was officially turned over to the state of Alabama on 7 July 1964 and then towed from the Puget Sound to her permanent berth in Mobile, where she arrived on 14 September.

Admiral Smith: It was so silly, because we lost the last opportunity to have battleship meet battleship outside of the old fellows down at Surigao Strait, south of Leyte. We missed the last opportunity when Halsey took the Third Fleet off—they went off to the north and let the Japs come on out of the Philippines. That's another memory, though.

Paul Stillwell: Yes, indeed.
What do you recall about antiaircraft practice in the *Arizona*?

Admiral Smith: Pretty shabby. The 3-inch guns then weren't worth a damn. We had practice, and we didn't have radar, of course. The ship had very antiquated and very simple fire control procedures.

Paul Stillwell: What do you remember about those procedures?

Admiral Smith: I just remember very little about them, except that it's so complicated—unless you had a plane coming right at you, you couldn't possibly hit it. To hit the sleeve—I mean the towed sleeve, you couldn't possibly.

Paul Stillwell: So it was almost a seaman's eye or whatever.

Admiral Smith: Yes. So awful.
Even in World War II, the British antiaircraft fire was so hopelessly antiquated. I remember out with the British Far Eastern Fleet—I had destroyers out there for a period—and after I'd been out with the British fleet for a little bit and got acclimated, I asked the rear admiral D—destroyers—if I might have a towed target practice. I said, "My ships haven't had a director practice. All I want to do is to fire one gun at the sleeve for each of my ships. Because they hadn't had director practice at something moving like that out there in Trincomalee, out in Ceylon.

So he said, "Yes. Old boy, I'd like to come with you." So he came out, and we proceeded to sea and out came a tow plane, towing a sleeve, and I told the flagship *Dunlap* to fire one gun only. This was a practice for the director, not the guns. And about the third shot, the *Dunlap* shot the sleeve down. And the rear admiral said, "Pick up that sleeve, old boy, I've never seen one shot down." So that's just a comparison. It was just a question of money. They didn't have the finances to put in that kind of thing.

Paul Stillwell: Well, they didn't have radar, and they probably didn't have the proximity fuze either.

Admiral Smith: No. We had rather perfect firing, I thought, in those days. Course, it's all gone now; you've got missiles.

Paul Stillwell: What do you recall about the *Arizona* towing targets? Did you have rake parties on the fantail?[*]

Admiral Smith: Yes, I wasn't involved in that, so I just don't remember. I never got myself involved in it. Yes, she had rake parties and I was never a part of it, though.

Paul Stillwell: Had the *Procyon* been involved in any of that work?

Admiral Smith: No, no. Nothing of that sort. *Procyon* was the flagship of the train.[†] I started out as the radio officer for the group—they call it the communication officer now—for the rear admiral. And Arleigh Burke took up that same job later on. That was not a terribly interesting experience, though.

Paul Stillwell: I interviewed one of your classmates when he was still alive, Thomas Dyer, who had a turret officer job in the *Pennsylvania*.[‡]

Admiral Smith: Yes, Tommy went on into intelligence, of course.

---

[*] "Raking" was a method of measuring the fall of shot in relation to the target—how much short, how much long. It was done from a boat at the same range as the target was from the firing ship, though separated in bearing. The measuring device had vertical pegs rising from a horizontal piece, thus giving the appearance of an upside-down garden rake.
[†] The fleet train was the term used then to describe the service and support ships. She was flagship of Commander Fleet Base Force, a rear admiral.
[‡] See the Naval Institute oral history of Captain Thomas H. Dyer, USN (Ret.).

Paul Stillwell: Code breaking.

Admiral Smith: Yes. And I think he was rather good at it.

Paul Stillwell: Very good, apparently.

Admiral Smith: Yes. Another classmate of mine, Eddie Layton was also—he was Admiral Nimitz's—I just . . .*

Paul Stillwell: He was the Pacific Fleet intelligence officer.

Admiral Smith: Yes.

Paul Stillwell: He had started out with Admiral Kimmel and then he moved on with Admiral Nimitz.†

Admiral Smith: Poor old Kimmel. He was hog-tied. You know, Joe Richardson, who was turned over to Kimmel, tried desperately to get the Pacific Fleet brought back to the West Coast.‡ And he insisted that Roosevelt retired him.§ So Kimmel couldn't bring the fleet anywhere else.

Paul Stillwell: Right.

Admiral Smith: Stuck with it.

Paul Stillwell: That was the price Richardson paid for being prescient.

---

* See the Naval Institute oral history of Rear Admiral Edwin T. Layton, USN (Ret.).
† Admiral Husband E. Kimmel, USN, served as Commander in Chief Pacific Fleet from 1 February 1941 to 17 December 1941. Fleet Admiral Chester W. Nimitz, USN, served as Commander in Chief Pacific Fleet from 31 December 1941 to 24 November 1945.
‡ Admiral James O. Richardson, USN, served as Commander in Chief U.S. Fleet (CinCUS) from 6 January 1940 to 1 February 1941.
§ Franklin D. Roosevelt served as President of the United States from 4 March 1933 until his death on 12 April 1945.

Admiral Smith: Yes.

Paul Stillwell: How sophisticated were the damage control procedures in the *Arizona*?

Admiral Smith: I know we drilled at it quite heavily, but I was never part of that business. Of course, the engineers, and certain areas of the 5-inch battery were involved in it, but I was never involved in the damage control procedures. If you'd presumably taken a torpedo hit, you could put wire-screen torpedo nets over the side and try to plug up the hole. And that's getting a little dim, but I do remember that we had torpedo nets and the stuffing went into the supposed hole. I don't think any of them ever took a torpedo hit, though. I don't think any of our battleships ever took torpedo hits, not that I recall.

Paul Stillwell: Well, except at Pearl Harbor.[*]

Admiral Smith: Yes, but nowhere out at sea, I don't think. In *Missouri* supposedly it would take six torpedo hits on the side.

Paul Stillwell: That's remarkable.

Admiral Smith: Now the *Arizona*, with her new blisters probably would have taken three or four hits without capsizing, without really losing the ship.

Paul Stillwell: The *Arizona* had two different systems for steering, the steam and the electrical. Do you have any recollections of the virtues of each of those?

Admiral Smith: The steam steering engine was very, very good. I do know that we also had hand steering in her. You could rig up a device down in the steering engine room

---

[*] On Sunday, 7 December 1941, Japanese carrier planes attacked and heavily damaged American warships at the naval base at Pearl Harbor, Hawaii. The U.S. Congress declared war on Japan the following day.

and put crews down there to work on the device that could turn the rudders. That sort of failed too.

Paul Stillwell: But in your recollection, the steam was pretty commonly used?

Admiral Smith: Commonly used and very successful. In my destroyer, the *Stewart*, the battle around Bali Island, we took a shell hit from the Japs right in the steering engine room. And the steering engine—I flooded two void spaces forward, two peak tanks forward, to raise the stern as much as possible, but let the engine keep on running. And it ran in water. It got me on back into Surabaya.*

Paul Stillwell: I didn't know it could do that.

Admiral Smith: It did. The steam lines were not damaged, and the engine worked all right, got me back.

Paul Stillwell: I guess a lot of the auxiliary machinery in the *Arizona* was run by steam, such as the boat cranes and what have you. Probably fire pumps.

Admiral Smith: Yes. I've forgotten so much about that ship.

Paul Stillwell: Well, it's not like you have to take a test on it.

Admiral Smith: [Chuckle] No.

Paul Stillwell: What do you remember about the bridge layout. Was that pretty comfortable?

---

* After taking damage the *Stewart* was dry-docked in Surabaya, Java, where she was captured by the Japanese.

Admiral Smith: Yes, it was. I do remember that it wasn't a hell of a big bridge. You could see well from either wing of the bridge. You could see well to the stern, as I recall, which you could not do on *Missouri*. You couldn't see around all the superstructure. But the *Arizona*, I think you could see very well astern, so that you could see whether some ship was creeping up on you, or whatever.

Paul Stillwell: Apparently it had been open to the elements earlier in the '20s, and was enclosed.

Admiral Smith: Well, we had bridge windows. I do recall that in fog—now, you mentioned fog—you'd bring down the bridge windows and stick your neck out and look. And you had visual lookouts in the wings of the bridge. And if you needed, you put lookout in the eyes of the ship, in the bow. But in firing the guns, now, all the bridge windows were rolled down.

Paul Stillwell: Did you ever operate the ship from the conning tower?

Admiral Smith: It could be done, but it was pretty unhandy. In the *Missouri* I did once, just for the hell of it. Just operated through the conning tower. But never in *Arizona*. I don't ever remember that. I do think that at general quarters in the *Arizona*, the navigator proceeded to the conning tower with the captain, of course. So I don't think I ever was in there.

Paul Stillwell: I saw a report from the first captain back in 1916-18, and he said that he had a real problem with visibility from the conning tower.[*]

Admiral Smith: Oh, yes.

Paul Stillwell: Because the bridge itself, aft of that, obstructed the view.

---

[*] Captain John D. McDonald, USN, commanded the *Arizona* from 17 October 1916 to 18 February 1918.

Admiral Smith: You could only see, maybe about, say, 135 degrees; you couldn't see around 180.

Paul Stillwell: Right.

Admiral Smith: Probably 45 degrees abaft of beam was about all you could see out of the conning tower, something like that.

Paul Stillwell: Maybe not even that much.

Admiral Smith: But maybe not, no.

Paul Stillwell: What do you recall about replenishment? The Arizona had done some experiments with underway replenishment in the '20s.

Admiral Smith: We probably did it, but I don't ever recall going alongside a tanker in the *Arizona*.

Paul Stillwell: I think they had the bow-to-stern method, where the oiler would trail a hose.

Admiral Smith: I don't recall ever refueling at sea in the *Arizona*. *Missouri* did frequently. And that was really—well, I got a lot of stories about—I think I already told you about those. That was easy. With some guys—they don't mess up. But I don't recall the *Arizona*, no.

Paul Stillwell: I think those were probably just some isolated experiments.

Admiral Smith: Now in *Farragut* destroyer, where I was a gunnery officer, we fueled from tankers. We tried several experiments there too. I think they'd have the tanker put a bowline on them, then they'd shear out a little bit just to hold it. But then we decided that was stupid, so we were set free, come alongside, hook up hoses and steam carefully. But I do know we experimented with being towed by a line from the tanker on back just forward of the bridge I think we hooked onto the bollards there and be towed out.

Paul Stillwell: In the late '30s, the *Arizona* refueled some destroyers that way just before the war started.

Admiral Smith: Could be, I just don't remember ever seeing one or not.

Paul Stillwell: What do you recall about fleet problems while you were in the *Arizona*?

Admiral Smith: I know we had them, but I just don't remember anything about it. As officer of the deck you steamed in some formation, and somebody told you what the formation would be, but I don't remember anything about it.

Paul Stillwell: And simulated firing at the simulated enemy.

Admiral Smith: Yes, yes. Well, it gave the flag officers some little practice, but didn't make a bit of difference to us officers of the deck. You just steamed the ship where it had to go.

Paul Stillwell: Well, and I suppose they were testing doctrine. The *Langley* was just coming into the fleet and seeing how aircraft could fit in.[*]

Admiral Smith: Yes, at the *Arizona* time that was going to be the main battle line. Next one, the *Saratoga* came along and started to change things real quickly.[†] It was slow to

---

[*] USS *Langley* (CV-1) was originally commissioned as the collier *Jupiter* (AC-3) in 1913 with Commander Joseph M. Reeves, USN, in command. She was later converted to the U.S. Navy's first aircraft carrier. She was commissioned as the *Langley* in 1922 with Commander Kenneth Whiting, USN, in command.

[†] USS Saratoga (CV-3), a *Lexington*-class aircraft carrier, was commissioned 16 November 1927. She had a standard displacement of 33,000 tons, was 888 feet long, 106 feet in the beam, an extreme width of 130 feet on the flight deck, and had a draft of 24 feet. She had a top speed of 33.5 knots and could accommodate approximately 60-70 aircraft. She was originally armed with eight 8-inch guns that were later removed in World War II.

catch on, but it did—even before Midway.*

Paul Stillwell: Right.

Well, do you remember anything about ship-to-ship athletics, like boxing, wrestling, the race-boat crews?

Admiral Smith: Yes, everybody had a race-boat crew. And I don't remember if the *Arizona* had a good one. I can remember race-boat crews, and I do remember the *California* usually won and *Tennessee*. I don't remember whether *Arizona* had a good crew—why, I don't know. I think if you collected a good crew, you kept them. Promoted them and kept them on board ship, I guess, because it was very important to win the crew races.

Paul Stillwell: Well, I've heard this complaint from some of the sailors who were in the ship in the '30s, that the athletes were given preferential treatment and better promotions.

Admiral Smith: Oh, no question. And the boxers—boxing team. But we had no sports except this crew and the boxing, of course, and wrestling.

Oh, I don't recall ever taking much part in those. The athletic officer was, usually, an important young fellow, whoever it might be. Very frequently the naval aviator was the athletic officer.

Paul Stillwell: That's interesting. This enlisted man remembered that the *Arizona* had an enlisted aviator, at least one. He said it was a chief named Darling.

Admiral Smith: Yes, yes, yes. And what'd they call them, had a special name?

Paul Stillwell: Aviation pilots.

---

* From 4 to 6 June 1942, U.S. and Japanese naval forces fought a battle northwest of Midway Island in the Pacific. After Japanese bombers had struck the island, carrier-based U.S. dive-bombers attacked and sank the Japanese carriers *Hiryu*, *Soryu*, *Kaga*, and *Akagi* and the cruiser *Mikuma*. U.S. ships lost were the carrier *Yorktown* (CV-5) and the destroyer *Hammann* (DD-412). The battle was both a tactical and strategic victory for U.S. forces.

Admiral Smith: Aviation pilot.

Paul Stillwell: APs.

Admiral Smith: Chief AP, yes. They were very good. No reason why they shouldn't be. You didn't have to have an engineering degree to be a pilot, just had to be damn good.

Paul Stillwell: hat do you remember about liberty ports in the Caribbean—Haiti, Panama?

Admiral Smith: Panama—of course, we were there. And had the usual problem that the crew had to get back at a certain hour, and you'd have some fights down on the dock with some taking on more rum than they could handle. But they were all handled quietly enough; maybe shore patrol had to bat a few heads with a stick, but usually it quelled all right. Others would take care of it.

Paul Stillwell: Well, and they keep them from smuggling the booze back aboard ship too.

Admiral Smith: Yes, you inspected. You carefully watched them as they came aboard. In the sailor's white dress, you couldn't very well carry a bottle of whiskey. And I think that if any excitement was ashore, they would never any aboard ship. And even in the *Missouri* time, I never had a case of drunkenness aboard ship, never had a case of drugs or any kind, never had a homosexual problem—nothing. It just didn't happen.

Paul Stillwell: It was a different era.

Admiral Smith: Different era.

Paul Stillwell: And I hope, maybe, that the *Missouri* got a better cut of men than most ships too.

Admiral Smith: She did. Strangely enough, she had a good crew. I don't think it was specially selected, but they were good. I'm going to have dinner with them tomorrow night.

Paul Stillwell: I know that will be a pleasure for you.

Admiral Smith: Well, I don't know. I'm a little concerned whether I should do this or not, because I don't know those men now. I've forgotten faces, and I think—I just think this because I live here—that they would be unhappy if I didn't show up.

Paul Stillwell: Well, they will be very happy that you will, because I've been to one or two of those, and the skipper is always revered. They ignore the fact that he later became an admiral—he's still the skipper.

Admiral Smith: Yes, yes. One called me last night, as a matter of fact, a former sailor from the *Stewart*. And he said he had my picture in his room. [Laughter] Now, that was a long time ago.

Paul Stillwell: Do you remember standing in-port watches in the *Arizona*?

Admiral Smith: Yes, we stood a day's duty. There would be usually 16 watch officers—might be down to 12, but with 16, you could stand, real easy. But with three you did two eight-hour watches on the day, no problem. You get your feet bigger—pounding pitch, we called them. My feet grew another size or so.

Paul Stillwell: I had a letter from Admiral Burke, who said that on his duty days, his wife would walk back and forth with him on the quarterdeck during those watches.

Admiral Smith: During my time, no. Arleigh could do anything, I guess. He's quite a guy. [Laughter]

Paul Stillwell: Yes, indeed he is.

Admiral Smith: I haven't seen him in so long, long time. I have some very fond memories of old Arleigh, though. I was just one year behind him; I was out of the class of '24, and he's '23. And we could have some arguments. And he'd listen to you, too, and then he'd knock it down if he didn't like it. But he listened; he was a good man—he is a good man. A good CNO.

Paul Stillwell: What do you recall about the ship's visits to San Francisco?

Admiral Smith: Almost nothing of any consequence. I know that we—I know my last trip to San Francisco with my wife we had some nice Italian meals. Nothing special, though. Nothing memorable that I recall.

Paul Stillwell: Anything about the ports up around Puget Sound?

Admiral Smith: Puget Sound was quite different. Those were—they're so different: Port Angeles, Port Townsend, and Bremerton, Seattle. Seattle itself. Quite different—people and places.

Paul Stillwell: Pleasant place to go in the summer.

Admiral Smith: Very pleasant, very pleasant—always.

Paul Stillwell: Do you have any memory of Navy yard time from Bremerton?*

Admiral Smith: Yes, we went into Bremerton in the *Arizona*, I believe, the fall of 1928. I think we were up there for three months' overhaul and very successful. Brought her home. Everything went nicely. We in the turrets didn't have any problems; we did our own overhauling of the turrets. Overhaul is always with the ship's machinery, I guess.

---

* Puget Sound Navy Yard, Bremerton, Washington.

Paul Stillwell: It's interesting that she would get an overhaul that soon before her really extensive rebuilding program at Norfolk.

Admiral Smith: Yes. We had three months and six weeks. The interval overhaul would be six weeks, and the main overhaul would be three months. No, that overhaul in Norfolk was a year.

Paul Stillwell: Some of these carriers and their modernization, it goes a lot longer than that.

Admiral Smith: Well, they're talking about modernizing one of the carriers. I've heard it mentioned it's going to be at tremendous expense, though, for modernization.

Paul Stillwell: Well, the *Enterprise* is . . .

Admiral Smith: *Enterprise* is one of them I'm thinking about. If they're going to refuel her and put in new—it's going to be very expensive.[*]

Paul Stillwell: Yes, indeed.

Admiral Smith: But the battleship brought back something around $400 million for the overhaul.[†] And the *Missouri* was built for $100 million.

Paul Stillwell: Right.

Admiral Smith: I suppose the *Wisconsin* will have a chance to fire something over there in the Persian Gulf, but that's awfully close quarters for her maneuver.[‡] But I wouldn't

---

[*] The nuclear-powered aircraft carrier *Enterprise* (CVN-65) was overhauled from 1990 to 1994 at Newport News Shipbuilding and Dry Dock Company.
[†] The *Missouri* was reactivated and modernized at the Long Beach Naval Shipyard from 1984 to 1986.
[‡] Both the *Missouri* and her sister ship *Wisconsin* (BB-64) operated in the Persian Gulf during Operation Desert Storm in 1991. They fired both missiles and 16-inch projectiles.

put that aircraft carrier, *Independence*, in there. Get her out. She hasn't got room enough to move at all. That's awfully stupid, I think, but then I'm not running that war.

I won't tell you what I think about it, but two of my nieces were in here not long ago. They wanted to know, and I told them what I would do. And both of them said they're glad I'm not having anything to do with it. [Laughter]

Paul Stillwell: What do you recall about communications in the *Arizona*?

Admiral Smith: Didn't have anything to do with it. I know that as far as flag signals and semaphores, and so on, all went very nicely. I don't recall ever having any problem. Never involved in it.

Paul Stillwell: What do you recall about loading ammunition?

Admiral Smith: That's rather simple. It's a very safe procedure. All hands' job, of course. Smoking lamps out. Everybody there just as if they're at general quarters. And all sorts of safety precautions, safety procedures till the powder's stored below and the shells stored below and latched up safe and secure. Then smoking lamps lighted.

We paid close attention to safety. It just utterly amazed me about the *Iowa*. I was sitting here and the phone rang on the day of the explosion. A young woman said, "I want to talk to you on the Navy about the *Iowa* explosion."

I said, "What?" She wanted to interview me because the *Iowa* just had the turret explosion, and I said, "I don't know anything about it."

She said, "I know, but I'm told that you had command of one of the sister battleships, and you could tell me—"

I said, "Look, honey, I could sketch and describe that turret, but I ain't going to tell you about what happened. I don't know."

She said, "Well, sorry to bother you." [Laughter] Some young reporter—reporteress.

Paul Stillwell: You talked about the landing force. Did you take that field piece ashore?

Admiral Smith: Yes, we had a little 3-inch popgun.

Paul Stillwell: Who fired that? The gunner's mates?

Admiral Smith: Yes. The gunner's mates worked on it. There would be probably the saluting battery crew.

Paul Stillwell: I see.

Admiral Smith: Same people.

Paul Stillwell: Did you have mock battles ashore?

Admiral Smith: No, no, not really. I think once—come to think about it, we did have one company of infantry would be off and have some sort of attack. All pretty stupid, we thought. [Laughter]

Paul Stillwell: I think I've run out of my questions. Let me look through the list.

Admiral Smith: As I say, my memory's so poor about that ship, that I can't—I'm not any help to you.

Paul Stillwell: Well, I don't agree with that assessment at all. I see in the spring of '28, you went out to Hawaii. What do you recall about that cruise?

Admiral Smith: Spring of '28, yes. My wife went out, and we had an apartment. And Tom Turner and I had shared an apartment, and our wives did some cooking for us. Tom Turner's dead now. I remember some of the junior officers I stood watches with. I remember on a midwatch out in Honolulu, that warm atmosphere, just as calm as could be, you had trouble staying awake from 12:00 to 4:00 at night.

Paul Stillwell: It's bad enough being up then anyway.

Admiral Smith: Yes.

I just thought of a—Pfingstag was one of the young ensigns on the ship.* Used to be my junior officer when I was watch officer. I wonder what's become of him. He was a fine, young man. Two of them, two brothers.

Paul Stillwell: Apparently, there was still a bar across the channel entrance, because the log shows the ship going into Honolulu rather than Pearl Harbor.

Admiral Smith: We anchored off Honolulu, I think. I remember there was a problem there of rolling heavily. One of the ships rolled so badly that some damage occurred. If you anchored just before you hit the bar, just short of that, a ship would get to where she'd roll heavily. I don't remember having difficulty ourselves in *Arizona*, but one of the ships did. *Maryland*, I think. I remember it took some damage. Why, I don't know.

But Pearl Harbor was such a silly place to keep a fleet with the onset of war. It's just unbelievable.

Paul Stillwell: Well, the ship went out to Lahaina for some time also.

Admiral Smith: Yes, Lahaina Roads, and we anchored out there in some tremendously deep anchorage. We had to walk out the anchor. And I remember the water was so clear in Lahaina Roads, you could see sharks look like minnows, practically, on the bottoms. It was very clear water.

Paul Stillwell: You'd walk it out rather than drop out?

Admiral Smith: Oh, yes, we'd just walk out the anchor.

---

* Ensign Carl J. Pfingstag, USN.

Paul Stillwell: Well, as a matter of fact, I see that the ship was out there quite a little while there in May and June.

Admiral Smith: It was in connection with a fleet exercise, of course.

Paul Stillwell: Then you went up to Puget Sound area. Oh, here's a division commander on board, Admiral Upham, later the Asiatic Fleet commander.*

Admiral Smith: Yes. Upham, yes. And it had to be a short period. I don't think he was on board any length of time. It must have been because his flagship went into temporary overhaul.†

Paul Stillwell: Then you went to Panama and Cuba. Any memories of Cuba?

Admiral Smith: We didn't go to Havana; we just went to Guantánamo. That's when I told you about the Ward K. Wortman and his gig coxswain. [Laughter]

Paul Stillwell: And then you went to Norfolk and put her in dry dock.

Admiral Smith: That was it.

Paul Stillwell: Well, anything I didn't think to ask about, Admiral?

Admiral Smith: As I say, my memory's failing in so many of those things. I think that you tend to remember the events of World War II more than anything that happened before or since.

Missouri, I don't remember so many details. I do remember the fun of having the ship. That's the biggest memory I have—how much fun it was to have her. She was a gorgeous thing, too, and so pretty.

---

* Rear Admiral Frank B. Upham, USN, Commander Battleship Division Three.
† Upham's regular flagship was the *Pennsylvania* (BB-38).

Paul Stillwell: A kind of satisfaction that you couldn't get from the *Arizona*, because she didn't have near the power.

Admiral Smith: No way, no. As officer of the deck on *Arizona*, I could handle that ship all right—how to manage her in column or turning with the rest of the ships—keeping the turning circle exactly right. That was easy enough, which you had to know and had to remember the effect of where was the sea coming from, and so and so and so and so. But the *Missouri* was just so much power. Handled just like a destroyer.

Paul Stillwell: Well, and the *Missouri* had two rudders instead of one also.

Admiral Smith: Yes, yes.

You know, one strange thing about the Missouri—I get back to her. You couldn't back her—you couldn't see her going astern. I remember once in Guantánamo with *Missouri*, we were anchored, and she was headed upstream on the ebb tide. And I tried to turn her in a rather narrow turning area that you had there with her in Guantánamo Bay. She didn't respond at all, so I backed her out. And I got a signal from the watchtower saying, "Is that a Weehawken ferry?" I backed her out much easier. And you backed with engines; you didn't back her with the rudders.

Paul Stillwell: I talked to Tiny McCorkle, who said he did that down there, because there wasn't much room to turn around.*

Admiral Smith: Yes.

McCorkle, I hadn't thought of him in years and years.

Paul Stillwell: He lives near Annapolis now.

---

* Captain Francis D. McCorkle, USN, commanded the USS *New Jersey* (BB-62) from 17 November 1951 to 20 October 1952.

Admiral Smith: I relieved him as chief of staff Destroyers Atlantic Fleet in 1950 in Newport. Tiny was a big fellow, a good man too.

Paul Stillwell: I just had a visit a few weeks ago from Rear Admiral Bob Erly.* He said that McCorkle really had a useful influence on his career. Said he needed to get some Washington time in to get the visibility and exposure.

Admiral Smith: Bob Erly is a good man. I haven't seen him in some time either. He was here about three years ago. We had him in for a drink and meal or something. But Bob and Lois—very attractive young people. He came on as a rear admiral out at SACLant after I had retired.† I guess he was assistant chief of staff, or deputy chief of staff.

Paul Stillwell: I think he had an inspector general type job.

Admiral Smith: Yes, he had that later. He didn't have the total Navy job, I don't think, did he?

Paul Stillwell: I don't remember.

Admiral Smith: The man that had it so long was Bulkeley.‡ There was another good man—a torpedo boater.

Paul Stillwell: I talked to the man who was the deputy, I guess, CinCLant about the time Erly was there, was Dick Ashworth.§

---

* Rear Admiral Robert B. Erly, USN (Ret.), who has been interviewed for a Naval Institute oral history.
† Admiral Smith served as Supreme Allied Commander Atlantic, Commander in Chief Atlantic, and Commander in Chief Atlantic Fleet from 30 April 1963 to 30 April 1965.
‡ Rear Admiral John D. Bulkeley, USN, began serving as president of the Board of Inspection and Survey in 1967, continued after his age-mandated retirement in 1974, and remained until he finally left active duty in 1988 and was promoted to vice admiral.
§ Vice Admiral Frederick L. Ashworth, USN, was involved in the atomic bomb development in World War II. During the mission of 9 August 1945 against Nagasaki, Japan, Ashworth was the weaponeer on board the B-29 "Bocks Car."

Admiral Smith: Ashworth, yes. A brilliant man. He was one of the, almost a scientist on atomic weapons. Who was the number-one man there?

Paul Stillwell: Deak Parsons.*

Admiral Smith: Deak Parsons, yes, a wonderful guy. I knew him—two years ahead of me at the Naval Academy. Wonderful man. And they tell the story that he couldn't be trusted with his family money. He spent it on new equipment of some sort. His wife had to take charge of the finances to keep food and clothing in the house. [Laughter] But Deak had such a wonderful inventive mind. Very good. I knew him in the battleship *Idaho* in 1924. I never served with him again, although I guess he came across my field of vision when we had the new destroyers, the *Farragut* and *Dewey* and *Monaghan*.† He came out of the Bureau of Ordnance and was very, very critical of the new destroyers' fire control system, because so many things had to be done yet. And he was right. We hadn't anywhere near yet what we should. The old firetron control, and they were still sort of elementary. But it was only a couple of years when we had good ones.

As I recounted, the *Farragut* was 348, *Dunlap* was 384. And in that period of time, the gunnery was so good. I told you about hitting on the first salvo at 15,000 yards.

Paul Stillwell: Thomas Dyer was in the *New Mexico* when you were in the *Idaho*. And he told me about making that cruise down to Australia and New Zealand and what a pleasure that was.

Admiral Smith: I didn't make that one. I got transferred out of the *Idaho* into the *Procyon*. I didn't make that one.

---

* Captain William S. Parsons, USN, was involved in the development of the atomic bomb in New Mexico. During the mission of 6 August 1945, Parsons was the weaponeer on board the B-29 named "Enola Gay" that dropped the bomb on Hiroshima, Japan.
† The first of the "gold-platers," the modern destroyers designed in the 1930s, was the USS *Farragut* (DD-348), commissioned 18 June 1934. They replaced the old four-pipers as the front-line destroyers in the U.S. Fleet.

My admiral left and went down on another ship, and *Procyon* came back to the West Coast. I was left in the *Procyon*; the skipper put me to work at being the first division officer.

And I remember when—this has nothing to do with *Arizona* but a funny thing. When we got under way to head back to the United States, the captain and the navigator got into a fight—a real argument. The captain was named Orr, and the navigator was Bertram David—an old mustang, a tough old fellow too.[*] I liked him. And they got in such an argument that the captain started hollering at the navigator and tell him he was a dog-barking navigator. He didn't like the way he'd taken his departure bearings. And he said he was going to get one of those bright, young ensigns up there to be a navigator. So I became a navigator of the ship. Well, that was easy enough. An ensign right out of the Naval Academy can navigate all right, but I never had the job of navigator. I navigated the ship back to San Francisco and did all right too. And then he kept me on, and he kept me on as navigator until we went around to the East Coast in the *Procyon* in 1927. We got a new captain on board, Max Mike Frucht.[†] He was the oldest, most ancient of all the mustangs up from the ranks. And one of the lieutenants got in to make him the navigator and make me his assistant. I got a couple of good stories about that, but you don't want to hear them now. Admiral Marvell was the flag officer then.

Paul Stillwell: He was the former skipper of the *Arizona*.[‡]

Admiral Smith: Yes, sure he was, sure. Admiral Marvell. And his chief of staff, I remember came up on the bridge just wandering around. He had, oh, half a dozen ships or more in this formation. He said, "Now, navigator, I'd like to have a very careful fix. Tonight we'll go through Crooked Island Passage. I want a very careful fix so we navigate those waters carefully."

"Yes, sir."

---

[*] Commander Henry A. Orr, USN; Lieutenant Bertram David, USN, a former enlisted man.
[†] Captain Max M. Frucht, USN.
[‡] Captain George R. Marvell, USN, commanded the *Arizona* (BB-39) from 24 December 1921 to 27 July 1922. The *Procyon* was his flagship as Commander Fleet Base Force and Train Squadron Two in 1927.

Well, came sunset and starlight time, and by the greatest good luck, I had a five-star fix.* If you've never been a navigator, you wouldn't know, but when you get five separate stars all coming to a nice fix . . .

Paul Stillwell: That's remarkable.

Admiral Smith: It really is, because you had to take them fast, number one. And number two, they have to be well done too.

Paul Stillwell: Right.

Admiral Smith: I had a five-star fix. I'd just finished the fix on my chart board. The navigator had one, and I had one. Just finished when out came the chief of staff and Admiral Marvell. And the admiral said, "Navigator, do you my fix yet?"

"Not quite yet, sir."

So the chief of staff overlooked mine. He said, "Well, admiral, here's a good, excellent fix."

So the admiral came, "Yes, yes. Oh, splendid. Signal that out to the fleet then. This is the fix for 8:00 o'clock." That was the 8:00 o'clock fix to his squadron.

After they left the bridge, the navigator said to me, "From here on, I'll take the sights, and you work them out."

I said, "I ain't going to do that. I'm not going to do that."

"I tell you, I'm ordering you to do that."

I said, "No, way. Let's go to the captain." So we went to the captain, and I stayed navigator. I was an ensign; he was a lieutenant.

Paul Stillwell: Kind of embarrassing.

---

* In celestial navigation, individuals take sights of the angle above the horizon for various heavenly bodies. These angles are then used with a nautical almanac to compute lines of position on a chart. Where the lines of position intersect is called a "fix," the ship's position at the time of the sights.

Admiral Smith: You know, you can stand up for things. Right now we're having people not standing up for them—very senior people. Not standing up for what they know has to be done. That aircraft carrier in the Persian Gulf, absolute stupidity.

Paul Stillwell: It will be interesting to see how long that situation lasts. I mean, we got into this stalemate; now who knows what's going to happen?

Admiral Smith: I'm frightened; I'm really frightened.

Paul Stillwell: Saddam is crazy.* He had this dream the other night to point his missiles in the other direction.

Admiral Smith: This guy's crazy like a fox, and he's just a cruel and vicious bastard. I tell you, frankly, I wouldn't waste one battalion of infantry to save the lives of people in Iraq. I have mind of a certain other kind of weapon. We used it in Hiroshima to great effect. Saved lives, saved lives.

Paul Stillwell: This is why your nieces said they're glad you're not in charge. [Laughter]

Admiral Smith: Well, anybody who does it, if it came to that, would arouse the antagonism of the entire liberal world, but as time went by they'd forgive him when they understood it. Says I.

Paul Stillwell: Well, I'm about at the end of the tape, admiral. I'm really grateful for this opportunity to see you again.

Admiral Smith: Well, I do apologize . . .

Paul Stillwell: You need not.

---

* Saddam Hussein, authoritarian President of Iraq, took power in 1979. He led his nation into a war against Iran in the 1980s, and his forces invaded Kuwait in the summer of 1990. He was toppled from power after U.S. forces invaded Iraq in 2003. He was executed in 2006.

Admiral Smith: . . . for lack of memory; I can't remember about it.

Paul Stillwell: You are one of the very few officers I've spoken to who served in the ship in the '20s. Admiral Coffin was another, so I'm delighted to have the opportunity.

Admiral Smith: A long time ago, yes.

Launched in 1969, the U.S. Naval Institute's award-winning oral history program is among the oldest in the country. Used in combination with documentary sources, oral histories offer a richer understanding of naval history through candid recollections and explanations rarely entered into contemporary records. In addition, they help depict the atmosphere of a particular event or era in a manner not available in official documents.

The nonprofit Naval Institute accomplishes its history projects through contributed funds and gratefully accepts tax-deductible gifts of all sizes for this purpose. This support allows the Institute to preserve the life experiences of today's service men and women so they may enlighten and inspire future generations.

For information about opportunities to underwrite Naval Institute oral history projects, please contact the Naval Institute Foundation at 291 Wood Road, Annapolis, Maryland 21402; by phone at (410) 295-1054; or by e-mail at foundation@usni.org.

Index to the Oral History of
Admiral Harold Page Smith, U.S. Navy (Retired)

Alcohol
    Drinking by crew members of the battleship *Arizona* (BB-39) in the late 1920s, 100-101, 112

Antiair Warfare
    By ships of Destroyer Squadron Four with the British Eastern Fleet in 1944, 12, 103-104
    By ships of Destroyer Squadron Four at Iwo Jima in 1945, 11
    The battleship *Missouri* (BB-63) used drones in 1949-50 for antiaircraft target practice, 74

***Arizona*, USS (BB-39)**
    Enlisted men in the crew in the late 1920s, 73, 81-82, 87, 111-112
    Gunnery setup in the late 1920s, 78-79, 81, 87-93, 116
    Operations in the Pacific, Caribbean, and Atlantic in the late 1920s, 78-81, 87-93, 96, 104-120
    Ship handling in the late 1920s, 82-83
    Recreation, including sports, in the late 1920s, 86-87, 111
    Pet dogs, 88-89
    Spotter planes used by the ship in the 1920s, 93-95, 111-112
    Ship's boats, 81-82, 98
    Torpedo practice in the late 1920s, 101-102
    Extended overhaul and modernization at Norfolk Navy Yard, 1929-31, 81-84, 96-97, 115

Arliss, Captain Stephen H. T., Royal Navy
    Operations in the British Eastern Fleet in early 1944, 12

Blandy, Admiral William H. P., USN (USNA, 1913)
    In the early 1940s was Chief of the Bureau of Ordnance, 38
    As Commander in Chief Atlantic Fleet, spent time on board the battleship *Missouri* (BB-63) in 1949, 38-39

Brown, Captain William D., USN (USNA, 1924)
    Commanding officer of the battleship *Missouri* (BB-63) when she ran aground in January 1950, 29-31, 62

Budgetary Issues
    Disposal of spare ships and torpedoes in the 1950s and 1960s to save money for the Navy, 102

Burke, Admiral Arleigh A., USN (USNA, 1923)
   Served on board the battleship *Arizona* (BB-39) and fleet auxiliary *Procyon* (AG-11) as a junior officer in the 1920s, 78, 113

Byrd, Senator Harry F.
   Visited the battleship *Missouri* (BB-63) in the Caribbean in early 1950, 27-28

California, **USS (BB-44)**
   Scrapped in the 1950s to save money for the Navy, 103

Caloosahatchee, **USS (AO-98)**
   Refueling of the battleship *Missouri* (BB-63) in 1949, 7, 20

Ceylon
   Visited by ships of Destroyer Squadron Four in 1944, 12-13

Cherbourg, France
   In August 1949 the battleship *Missouri* (BB-63) anchored in the port during a midshipman training cruise, 17-25

Coffin, Ensign Clarence E. Jr., USN (USNA, 1927)
   On the rifle team of the battleship *Arizona* (BB-39) in the late 1920s, 88

Commercial Ships
   The British liners *Queen Elizabeth* and *Queen Mary* vied for space in Cherbourg, France, with the battleship *Missouri* (BB-63) in August 1949, 24-25

Congress, U.S.
   Senators and representatives visited the battleship *Missouri* (BB-63) in the Caribbean in early 1950, 27-28

Corman, Lieutenant Harry, USN (USNA, 1920)
   Duty in a destroyer off the coast of Turkey in the early 1920s, 79
   Served in the late 1920s in the battleship *Arizona* (BB-39), 79

Crosley, Captain Walter S., USN (USNA, 1893)
   Commanded the battleship *Idaho* (BB-42) in the mid-1920s, 98-99

Cummings, **USS (DD-365)**
   In August 1944 President Franklin D. Roosevelt rode the ship from Alaska to the state of Washington, 32-33

Dennison, Captain Robert L., USN (USNA, 1923)
   In the late 1940s served as President Harry S. Truman's naval aide, 4

Destroyer Squadron Four
    Operations with the British Eastern Fleet in early 1944, 11-13
    In August 1944 President Franklin D. Roosevelt rode the destroyer *Cummings* (DD-365) from Alaska to the state of Washington, 32-33
    As part of Task Group 38.1 during the October 1944 Battle of Leyte Gulf, 52-53
    At Iwo Jima in early 1945, 11

Disciplinary Matters
    Captain's mast on board the battleship *Arizona* (BB-39) in the late 1920s, 81-82
    Shortly before World War II, Smith suspended an officer who was late in returning to the destroyer *Stewart* (DD-224), 99
    Black newspaper reporters who rode the battleship *Missouri* (BB-63) in the summer in 1949 concluded that black sailors were treated fairly, despite a captain's mast for fighting, 23-24
    Men of the *Missouri*'s Marine detachment were taken to mast in 1950 for misbehavior ashore, 59-61

Drones
    Used by the battleship *Missouri* (BB-63) in 1949-50 for antiaircraft target practice, 74

Duke, Captain Irving T., USN (USNA, 1924)
    Commanded the battleship *Missouri* (BB-63) in 1950-51, 35-36, 75-76

Duncan, Admiral Donald B., USN (USNA, 1917)
    As Vice Chief of Naval Operations in 1951, had a hand in arranging Smith's first assignment as a flag officer, 69-70

***Dunlap*, USS (DD-384)**
    In early 1944 operated with the British Eastern Fleet, 11-12, 48, 95
    In August 1944 escorted President Franklin D. Roosevelt during a voyage from Alaska to the state of Washington, 32-33
    Gunfire support of the U.S. invasion of Iwo Jima in early 1945, 48, 95-96

Edwards, Rear Admiral Richard S., USN (USNA, 1907)
    Known for his loud voice, he served in World War II as deputy chief of staff to CominCh, 42-43

Enlisted Personnel
    In the battleship *Arizona* (BB-39) in the late 1920s, 73, 81-82, 87, 111-112
    Black newspaper reporters who rode the battleship *Missouri* (BB-63) in the summer in 1949 concluded that black sailors were treated fairly, despite a captain's mast for fighting, 23-24
    Men of the *Missouri*'s Marine detachment were taken to mast in 1950 for misbehavior ashore, 59-61
    The *Missouri*'s crew was capable but not handpicked, 67-68, 112-113

Fahrion, Rear Admiral Frank G., USN (USNA, 1917)
　　Served 1950-52 as Commander Destroyer Force Atlantic Fleet, 69

Fanning, **USS (DD-385)**
　　Gunfire support of the U.S. invasion of Iwo Jima in early 1945, 96

Farragut, **USS (DD-348)**
　　Underway replenishment experiments in the mid-1930s, 109-110

Fechteler, Admiral William M., USN (USNA, 1916)
　　In 1942 served in the Bureau of Naval Personnel, 41-42
　　As Commander in Chief Atlantic Fleet in 1950, was involved with the battleship *Missouri* (BB-63) after she had run aground and then been refloated, 30, 40-41

Flanigan, Captain Howard A., USN (Ret.) (USNA, 1910)
　　In the late 1920s was gunnery officer of the battleship *Arizona* (BB-39), 77-79
　　Served in London during World War II, 77

France
　　In August 1949 the battleship *Missouri* (BB-63) visited Cherbourg during a midshipman training cruise, 17-25

Fraser, Admiral Sir Bruce, Royal Navy
　　Was on board the battleship *Missouri* (BB-63) for the Japanese surrender in 1945 and visited again in England in 1949, 21-22

Frucht, Captain Max Mike, USN
　　Commanded the fleet auxiliary *Procyon* (AG-11) in the mid-1920s, 123

Great Britain
　　In June 1949 the battleship *Missouri* (BB-63) hosted British visitors in Portsmouth, England, during a midshipman training cruise, 17-22

Guadalcanal, Solomon Islands
　　In 1942 Admiral Ernest J. King pushed for a U.S. offensive at Guadalcanal, 43-44

Guantánamo Bay, Cuba, Naval Base
　　Intermediate stop for the battleship *Arizona* (BB-39) in 1929 on her way to Norfolk for modernization, 81-82
　　Training site for the battleship *Missouri* (BB-63) during operations in 1949-50, 8, 27, 37, 40, 46-47, 120

Gunnery-Naval
　　By the 14-inch turrets of the battleship *Arizona* (BB-39) in the late 1920s, 78-79, 87-93, 116
　　Arizona's saluting battery in the late 1920s, 81

In the battleship *Nevada* (BB-36), 1929-31, 83
Star shell duel between the destroyer *Dunlap* (DD-348) and ships of the British East Fleet in 1944, 47-48
Antiaircraft firing by ships of Destroyer Squadron Four in 1944-45, 11-12, 103-104
Gunfire support of the U.S. invasion of Iwo Jima in early 1945, 48-49, 95-96
Shore bombardment practice by the battleship *Missouri* (BB-63) in 1949-50 at Vieques, 10, 27-28
Drones were used by the *Missouri* in 1949-50 for antiaircraft target practice, 74
Missouri's shooting during the Korean War in the early 1950s, 68

HO3S
Sikorsky helicopter was used in a utility role by the battleship *Missouri* (BB-63) during 1949 operations, 22-23

Halsey, Fleet Admiral William F., Jr., USN (Ret.) (USNA, 1904)
Role as Commander Third Fleet during the October 1944 Battle of Leyte Gulf, 52-53
Funeral in Washington, D.C., on 20 August 1959, 50-52

Harbor Pilots
Role in guiding the battleship *Missouri* (BB-63) in 1949-50, 62-65

Hart, Admiral Thomas C., USN (USNA, 1897)
As Commander in Chief Asiatic Fleet, inspected the destroyer *Stewart* (DD-224) in 1940, 56-57

Hawaii
Operations by the battleship *Arizona* (BB-39) in the vicinity in 1928, 117-118

Helicopters
The Sikorsky HO3S was used in a utility role by the battleship *Missouri* (BB-63) during 1949 operations, 22-23

Honolulu, Hawaii
The battleship *Arizona* (BB-39) anchored there in 1928, unable to go into Pearl Harbor, 117-119

Idaho, **USS (BB-42)**
Operation of the ship's boats in the mid-1920s, 98-99

Iowa, **USS (BB-61)**
Turret explosion on board in April 1989, 89-90, 116

Iwo Jima, Bonin Islands
Naval gunfire support of the U.S. invasion in early 1945, 11, 48-49, 95-96

Johnson, Rear Admiral Felix L., USN (USNA, 1920)
    As Commander Destroyer Force Atlantic Fleet in 1948, asked Smith to be his chief of staff, 1-2

Kimberly, Captain Victor A., USN (USNA, 1899)
    Commanded the battleship *Arizona* (BB-39) from June to September 1928, 80

King, Admiral Ernest J., USN (USNA, 1901)
    Actions as Commander in Chief U.S. Fleet (CominCh) in 1942-43, 41-46

Kraker, Lieutenant George Patton, USN (USNA, 1920)
    Served in the late 1920s as plotting room officer in the battleship *Arizona* (BB-39), 78

Leadership
    Smith's style as commanding officer of the battleship *Missouri* (BB-63) in 1949-50, 27-29, 73-75

Leave and Liberty
    For American midshipmen visiting England in the summer of 1949, 21

Leyte Gulf, Battle of
    Role of Admiral William F. Halsey, Commander Third Fleet, during the October 1944 battle, 52-53

Longfellow, Lieutenant (junior grade) William J., USN (USNA, 1924)
    Served as a turret officer in the battleship *Arizona* (BB-39) in the late 1920s, 78

Marine Corps, U.S.
    Detachment on board the battleship *Nevada* (BB-36) in 1929, 97-98
    Men of the Marine detachment of the battleship *Missouri* (BB-63) were taken to mast in 1950 for misbehavior ashore, 59-61

Marshall, General of the Army George C., USA
    Role in strategic planning for the 1944 invasion of Normandy, 44-45
    Died in October 1959, 50

Marvell, Rear Admiral George R., USN (USNA, 1889)
    Commanded the Fleet Base Force in the mid-1920s, 123-124

Matthews, Francis P.
    As Secretary of the Navy in late 1950, arranged for Smith to become Deputy Chief of Information, 69

Medical Problems
While commanding the battleship *Missouri* (BB-63) in 1949-50 Smith experienced pain from his sciatic nerve, 31-32

Mendenhall, Captain William K. Jr., USN (USNA, 1923)
Served as chief of staff to Commander Cruiser Force Atlantic Fleet during a midshipman cruise in 1949, 17, 20, 58

Millett, Commander John R., USN (USNA, 1936)
Operations officer of the battleship *Missouri* (BB-63) at the time of her grounding in January 1950, 37

Missouri, USS (BB-63)
In late 1948 Smith learned he would be commanding the ship, 1-2
Outward appearance in 1949 was marred by poor quality paint, 2-3, 13-14, 22, 58-59
By the late 1940s the size of the crew was well below World War II level, 2-4, 8-9, 36
Ship-handling qualities in 1949-50, 5-8, 28-29, 37, 63-65, 120
Operations in the Atlantic in 1949-50, 5-11, 14-15, 27-31, 39-40, 46-49, 54-55, 62-63, 66, 72, 74
Use of floatplanes and helicopters in 1949, 14-15, 22-23
Midshipman cruises in the summer of 1949, 15-26, 34, 57-58, 63-64, 75
Black newspaper reporters who rode the ship in the summer in 1949 concluded that black sailors were treated fairly, despite a captain's mast for fighting, 23-24
Enlisted personnel in the crew in 1949-50, 23-24, 59-61, 67-73, 112-113
Overhaul period at Norfolk Naval Shipyard in late 1949, 12-13, 64-65
Ran aground near Norfolk in January 1950 because of faulty navigation, 3, 6, 31, 34-37, 66-67
The grounding had no effect on the *Missouri*'s speed, 39-40
Gunnery in 1949-50, 10, 27-28, 47-48
Norfolk, Virginia, was the homeport for the ship in the late 1940s-early 1950s, 9-10, 54-57
Athletics among the ship's crew, 1949-50, 70-72
Shooting during the Korean War in the early 1950s, 68

Mountbatten, Admiral of the Fleet, Lord Louis, Royal Navy
As Supreme Allied Commander Southeast Asia in 1944, 12-13, 17, 45-46
As Britain's Chief of Defence Staff in the early 1960s, 12

Nash, Frank C.
Served 1953-54 as Assistant Secretary of Defense (International Security Affairs), 70

Naval Academy, Annapolis, Maryland
Summer cruises by midshipmen in the early 1920s, 5, 8

Naval Reserve, U.S.
Training of reservists on board the battleship *Missouri* (BB-63) in the late 1940s, 8-10

Navigation
Celestial navigation by the fleet auxiliary *Procyon* (AG-11) in the Caribbean in 1927, 123
In the crowded port of Cherbourg, France, in the summer of 1949, 24-25
The battleship *Missouri* (BB-63) ran aground near Norfolk in January 1950 because of faulty navigation, 3, 6, 31, 34-35

***Nevada*, USS (BB-36)**
Went back into active service in 1929 after modernization at the Norfolk Navy Yard, 83-84, 97-98

News Media
Black newspaper reporters who rode the battleship *Missouri* (BB-63) in the summer in 1949 concluded that black sailors were treated fairly, despite a captain's mast, 23-26
Coverage of the *Missouri* in early 1950, after she had been repaired following her grounding, 62

Nimitz, Fleet Admiral Chester W., USN (USNA, 1905)
In August 1959 attended the funeral of Fleet Admiral William Halsey in Washington, D.C., and asked consideration for promoting Admiral Raymond Spruance to five stars, 50-52

Norfolk, Virginia
Homeport for the battleship *Missouri* (BB-63) in the late 1940s-early 1950s, 9-10, 54-56

Norfolk Navy Yard, Portsmouth, Virginia
Extended modernization period for the battleship *Arizona* (BB-39), 1929-31, 81-84, 96-97
Overhauled the battleship *Missouri* (BB-63) in late 1949, 13
Repairs to the *Missouri* in February 1950 after she ran aground, 62

Normandy, France
Strategic planning for the 1944 invasion of Normandy, 44-45

Orr, Commander Henry A., USN (USNA, 1905)
Commanded the fleet auxiliary *Procyon* (AG-11) in the mid-1920s, 123

Panama
The battleship *Missouri* (BB-63) visited Cristobal in the spring of 1949, 49

Parsons, Lieutenant Commander William Sterling, USN (USNA, 1922)
    Served in the battleship *Idaho* (BB-42) in the mid-1920s, 122
    Concern about fire control in *Farragut* (DD-348)-class destroyers in the mid-1920s, 122

Peckham, Commander George E., USN (USNA, 1931)
    In 1949-50 served as executive officer of the battleship *Missouri* (BB-63), 3, 25, 28, 34-35, 74

Planning
    In 1942 Admiral Ernest J. King pushed for a U.S. offensive at Guadalcanal, 43-44
    Strategic planning for the 1944 invasion of Normandy, 44-45

Portsmouth, England
    In June 1949 the battleship *Missouri* (BB-63) hosted British visitors during a midshipman training cruise, 17-20

***Procyon*, USS (AG-11)**
    Operations in the mid-1920s, 84, 104, 122-124
    Served as flagship for Commander Fleet Base Force in the 1920s, 104, 123

Promotion of Officers
    In 1959, as Chairman of the House Armed Services Committee, Representative Carl Vinson declined a request to promote Admiral Raymond Spruance to five stars, 50-51

Puget Sound Navy Yard, Bremerton, Washington
    Overhauled the battleship *Arizona* (BB-39) in 1928, 114-115

Quebec Conference
    Issues at the Quadrant Conference in August 1943 involved the selection of Vice Admiral Louis Mountbatten as Supreme Commander Southeast Asia, 45-46

Racial Issues
    Treatment of black sailors on board the battleship *Missouri* (BB-63) in 1949, 23-26

Refueling at Sea
    Experiments involving the destroyer *Farragut* (DD-348) in the mid-1930s, 109-110
    Ship handling during 1949 replenishment between the battleship *Missouri* (BB-63) and the oiler *Caloosahatchee* (AO-98), 7, 20

Roosevelt, President Franklin D.
    In August 1944 rode the destroyer *Cummings* (DD-365) from Alaska to the state of Washington, 32-33

Royal Navy
    Operations of the British Eastern Fleet in early 1944, 11-12, 48, 95, 103-104

Ship Handling
    On board the battleship *Arizona* (BB-39) in the late 1920s, 82-83
    On board the battleship *Missouri* (BB-63) in 1949, 5-8, 28-29, 37, 63-64, 120

Smith, Rear Admiral Allan E., USN (USNA, 1915)
    In the summer of 1949, as Commander Cruiser Force Atlantic Fleet, was embarked in the battleship *Missouri* (BB-63), 15, 19-20, 24, 57-58
    Was involved in the aftermath of the grounding of the *Missouri* in early 1950, 30, 34-35

Smith, Admiral Harold Page, USN (Ret.) (USNA, 1924)
    Wife Dee, 12-13, 17, 25-27, 54, 114, 117
    As a Naval Academy midshipman in the early 1920s, 5, 8, 71
    First commissioned service was in the battleship *Idaho* (BB-42) in 1924-25, 98, 122
    Served in the crew of the fleet auxiliary *Procyon* (AG-11), 1925-28, 122-123
    Served as division officer in the battleship *Arizona* (BB-39) in 1928-29, 73, 77-120
    Service in the battleship *Nevada* (BB-36), 1929-31, 83-84
    As gunnery officer in the destroyer *Farragut* (DD-348), 1934-37, 109-110
    Commanded the destroyer *Stewart* (DD-224) from 1940 to 1942, 38, 56-57
    Rode in a heroes' parade in New York City in 1942, 41-42
    In 1942-43 served in the war plans section of the U.S. Fleet staff, 41-46, 77
    Commanded Destroyer Squadron Four in 1944-45, 11-12, 32-33, 52-53, 95-96, 103-104
    Commanded the battleship *Missouri* (BB-63) in 1949-50, 1-41, 47-48, 53-68, 70-76
    Served 1949-50 as chief of staff to Commander Destroyer Force Atlantic Fleet, 69, 120-121
    In 1950-51 was the Navy's Deputy Chief of Information, 69
    Served in the Office of the Secretary of Defense, 1951-53, 70
    Served in the Office of the Comptroller of the Navy, 1955-56, 102
    As Chief of Naval Personnel, 1958-60, 50-52
    Served 1960-63 as Commander in Chief U.S. Naval Forces Europe, 12

Spruance, Admiral Raymond A., USN (Ret.) (USNA, 1907)
    In August 1959 Fleet Admiral Chester Nimitz asked consideration for promoting Admiral Spruance to five stars, 50-51

***Stewart*, USS (DD-224)**
    Activities in 1940-41, before the outset of World War II, 56-57, 99
    Combat action around the Dutch East Indies in 1941-42, 38

Strategy
    In 1942 Admiral Ernest J. King pushed for a U.S. offensive at Guadalcanal, 43-44
    Strategic planning for the 1944 invasion of Normandy, 44-45

Swart, Captain Robert L., USN (USNA, 1924)
Supervised the overhaul of the battleship *Missouri* (BB-63) at Norfolk Naval Shipyard in late 1949, 13

Tarrant, Vice Admiral William T., USN (Ret.) (USNA, 1898)
Commanded the battleship *Arizona* (BB-39) from 1927 to 1929, 80-81
After he retired, met with Smith in Washington, 79-80

Tennessee, USS BB-43)
Scrapped in the 1950s to save money for the Navy, 103

Thach, Captain James H. Jr., USN (1923)
Commanded the battleship *Missouri* BB-63) in 1948-49, 2-6

Torpedoes
Torpedo practice by the battleship *Arizona* (BB-39) in the late 1920s, 101
Disposal of spare torpedoes from the Navy inventory in the 1950s, 102

Training
Of Naval Reservists on board the battleship *Missouri* (BB-63) in the late 1940s, 8-10
Midshipman cruises by the *Missouri* in the summer of 1949, 15-26
Training of the crew of the *Missouri* in early 1950 following the ship's grounding, 27-28, 47-48

Truman, President Harry S.
In late 1948 checked out Smith as potential commanding officer of the battleship *Missouri* (BB-63), 4
The *Missouri* stayed in commission as long as he was President, 50, 68

Turkey
A U.S. destroyer off Smyrna was overrun by Greek refugees in the early 1920s, 79

Vieques Island, Puerto Rico
Target for shore bombardment practice by the battleship *Missouri* (BB-63) in 1949, 10
Site of joint training maneuvers in 1950, 27-28

Vinson, Representative Carl (Democrat-Georgia)
In 1959, as Chairman of the House Armed Services Committee, declined a request to promote Admiral Raymond Spruance to five stars, 50-51

War Games
The battleship *Missouri* (BB-63) was involved in surface engagement games in the summer of 1949, 15-16

War Plans
    In 1942 Admiral Ernest J. King pushed for a U.S. offensive at Guadalcanal, 43-44
    Strategic planning for the 1944 invasion of Normandy, 44-45

Weather
    In August 1944 President Franklin D. Roosevelt rode the destroyer *Cummings* (DD-365) from Alaska to the state of Washington in rain and fog, 32-33

Willis, Admiral of the Fleet Sir Algernon, Royal Navy
    In June 1949, as Commander in Chief Portsmouth, welcomed the battleship *Missouri* (BB-63), 18-20

Wooldridge, Rear Admiral Edmund T., USN (USNA, 1920)
    Served in 1949-50 as Commander Destroyer Force Atlantic Fleet, 29-30, 40, 69

Wortman, Captain Ward K., USN (USNA, 1900)
    Commanded the battleship *Arizona* (BB-39) in 1928-29, 77, 79, 81-84, 119